For Lucy and Theo:
You are the best stories in my life.
And for P: I love you.

Praise For

"*Good Enough* is filled to the brim with hope. Wendi tells her story with a vulnerability and grace that brought me to tears more than once. This book invites us to stop striving to reach some unattainable level of godliness and instead see ourselves through God's eyes—with compassion and more love than we could ever imagine. As someone who struggles with anxiety and panic, I found reading Wendi's words to be deeply refreshing and comforting, like a cup of hot coffee on a freezing winter morning."

—Lauren Casper, author of *Loving Well in a Broken World*

"Wendi Nunnery offers freedom to women everywhere who have spent too much time striving to please God and not enough time resting in what he has already done for us. In a world that tells us all the ways we will never measure up, *Good Enough* is a refreshing glass of water for those who have exhausted themselves doing everything but resting in God's promises and love. With vulnerability and passion, Wendi reminds us that God wants so much more for us than striving to be perfect."

—Taylor Schumann, author and activist

"As a serial perfectionist, I've spent years trying to do enough, say enough, be enough, and perform enough to prove I am worthy of admiration and love. The rule-following and addiction to achievement is exhausting, which is why I'm so grateful to Wendi Nunnery for providing an escape route. *Good Enough* gives readers permission to stop striving for perfection and start living with holiness in view. If you're like me, you need this message."

—Jonathan Merritt, author of *Learning to Speak God from Scratch*

"There is an awakening happening. People are waking up to the idea that living a beautiful life often means letting go of the ridiculous standards put on them by others and by the culture at large. Wendi Nunnery is one of the people leading and writing on the front edge of this. In *Good Enough* she addresses the power of shame, the toxic expectations of others, caring for your own mental health, and what it means to get back to a faith where Jesus is enough. In the midst of a cultural moment with more confusion than clarity, her voice is exactly what is needed."

–B. T. Harman, writer, podcaster, creator of Blue Babies Pink

"These words are the very ones I most needed to hear. I am grateful for her gentle and open-hearted invitation into holiness over perfection, into belovedness over brokenness. Her willingness to go first and share her story (of faith, of motherhood, of mental battles, of marriage) gave me the freedom to explore more of my own evolving story, and I am confident that readers will experience the same gift in her words. Hearing her reminder that God's banner over me says *Good. Holy. Beloved. Called.* helped me remember what is true, and I will cling to that."

–Rachel Dawson,
writer, popular bookstagrammer, and host of *The RAD Podcast*

Good Enough

Learning to Let Go of Perfect
for the Sake of Holy

Wendi Nunnery

PARACLETE PRESS
BREWSTER, MASSACHUSETTS

2020 First Printing

Good Enough: Learning to Let Go of Perfect for the Sake of Holy

Copyright © 2020 by Wendi Nunnery

ISBN 978-1 64060-543-5

The Paraclete Press name and logo (dove on cross) are trademarks of Paraclete Press, Inc.

Library of Congress Cataloging-in-Publication Data
Names: Nunnery, Wendi, 1985- author.
Title: Good enough : learning to let go of perfect for the sake of holy /
    Wendi Nunnery.
Description: Brewster, Massachusetts : Paraclete Press, 2020. | Summary:
    "Good Enough tackles the lie that we are required to be perfect in order
    to be good and, most importantly, reveals the truth about how much we've
    already been given"— Provided by publisher.
Identifiers: LCCN 2020011858 (print) | LCCN 2020011859 (ebook) | ISBN
    9781640605435 (trade paperback) | ISBN 9781640605442 (epub) | ISBN
    9781640605459 (pdf)
Subjects: LCSH: Holiness. | Perfection—Religious aspects—Christianity.
Classification: LCC BT767 .N86 2020 (print) | LCC BT767 (ebook) | DDC
    234/.8--dc23
LC record available at https://lccn.loc.gov/2020011858
LC ebook record available at https://lccn.loc.gov/2020011859

10 9 8 7 6 5 4 3 2 1

Published by Paraclete Press
Brewster, Massachusetts
www.paracletepress.com

Printed in the United States of America

CONTENTS

Part Three
Undoing Perfect

Part Four
Receiving Holy

 **The first introduction to this book was a bit different from the one you're reading now.** A few years ago, I had an idea I felt compelled to share, a truth that had cracked me open and left me split in two halves: one half the little girl who grew into a young woman convinced that just one more right decision would settle her restless quest for perfection, and the other half a wife and mother who had finally learned why that quest was a magnificent waste of time.

As I put my fingers to the keyboard and began to write, I was unaware of what I would endure in the next two years or how the lesson I thought I'd already learned would continue to show up. It is a lesson for a lifetime, it seems, and this book is both a testament to the wisdom God has shared with me and an exploration of just how much more I have to learn.

Perhaps like yours, my whole life has been spent trying to live up to an impossible standard. While I've often been good at things, very rarely—if ever—have I been the best. I have lived an above-average existence in terms of what the world would label a success, and yet there is a constant sense that I don't measure up. I still walk around this beautiful life and wonder, "Why am I not doing this better?"

I have fallen hard for the lie that tells me perfection is the goal: for motherhood, marriage, friendship, work, health, and, most of all, for faith. I scorn myself for failure and then, once I've tired of that, run in the opposite direction and settle into the muck and mire as if I belong in it, as if simple acceptance of my flaws is all there is to life. I make a home in my mess, comfortable in the knowledge that being flawed means I don't have to expect so much of myself.

But that's not really satisfying either. That's just another kind of bondage.

I'm tired, to tell you the truth. I've been running in circles for a long time, like a dog chasing her tail, in an effort to be the person who never disappoints. I have sought to garner love and salvation from those who are not equipped to give it. The temptation to people please has danced right beside my desire to honor God, and I have pulled myself to pieces as I have switched from one to the other and back again. Right when I think I've got the answers all figured out, an unexpected hand gets dealt, and I wonder how much longer this house of cards I've created will hold up.

The fleeting pleasure of affirmation or a soothed ego only ever gives way to more striving, more chasing. I have followed all the most popular rules of my faith, never rocking the boat or making noise, and what I have to show for it is a beautiful, well-ordered existence and an inner life of turmoil. The most intimate, authentic pieces of my soul are guarded under lock and key for fear that if I let them out, my whole world will collapse. This is arrogant, I know. It's also the legacy of an evangelical culture quick to turn believers into performers. I play god because religion has taught me the rules and now I can execute them in my sleep, no actual God required.

I know what Jesus has done for me. My mind is fully aware of what his death and resurrection mean, but the knowledge doesn't always translate to action. Because of this disconnect between mind and spirit, I have too often settled into the bland, self-righteous pursuit of perfection where as long as I follow the rules, I can rest easy.

But rest never comes. There is always another expectation to meet, another sin I must grind out, another box to check. Perfection is a heavy burden to try to carry on our own. This was the first lesson of Eden. God's children mistook their own free will as an equal alternative to his love, convinced they could do better, could be perfect without him. Because God is good, he offered a way for us to be made whole again. Holy, as God intended, once more.

Perhaps you think of good enough as second best—second place— and if we're honest with ourselves, none of us like to come in second. (As a die-hard Atlanta Falcons fan, I can tell you this from experience.) The lesson that's been hard won for me as I've fought for my mental health and tried to make room for God to deconstruct my long-held convictions about what is good, better, and best is that, in Christ, the work is done. It is all finished.

We've heard that before, but let's talk more about what it means.

To be perfect is to be without flaws, without errors of any kind. Think of Perfection as a creature designed to answer every question and meet any need. She knows all the answers to our questions about God and the church. She is contoured and shaped to fit every beauty standard, and everyone loves Perfection from a distance. But up close, Perfection is incredibly boring and has no real concept of what's good.

Holiness is a whole other level of perfection, one that comes by way of grace, repentance, and relationship. It is not your morality, your knowledge of Scripture, or even the affirmation of your faith community; it is a gift given by love. Holiness is our transformation into the likeness of the Savior, and it comes to everyone who chooses to follow him. Perfection is what we try, and fail, to attain. Holiness is what we've already received.

Perhaps, like me, you are tired of wasting time. That's why this book is in your hands, and it's why I wrote it. I thought of you often when I put these words to paper, of the faith you believe requires perfection, of the exhaustion that trails your every step, of the wonder you've lost in the effort to never mess up. I don't know you personally, but if you're like me, then the cost of your striving has been immense. While things have often looked just fine on the surface, your internal world is one that has been driven by the perpetual fear of failure and sin. The potential for loss is always great when we put our faith in the wrong gods, especially the ones we create for ourselves.

Underneath all the pretension and dogma, we know that there is so much more to being a Jesus follower than what the church sometimes offers. We know the searing pain of addiction and loss, depression and divorce, infidelity and illness, and we keep it locked up because, collectively, we are still trying to steer the ship ourselves. We are still running after perfect when what we need, what we really want, is holy.

Whether you have been a believer your whole life or have walked in faith for just a few months, I hope that in this book you will meet a kindred spirit. I hope that as I learn to see myself as good enough, you will too. Not because we're settling for less than or denying that our souls long for more, but because we have already accepted good enough as the gift of Jesus's glory upon us, and there is nothing more incredible than that.

This book will not be perfect. That's kind of the point. Some of you will love it and a few of you will hate it. But there is one of you who will read this book and see herself reflected back in its pages. She will recognize her story in mine and come to learn, as I have had to learn, that devotion to the rules and faithfulness to God are sometimes two very different things. It's for this woman that I write. It's for this woman, and for all the women like her, that I pray.

These words are an invitation for us to be okay with our neediness and allow it to move us in a different, bolder direction. They are an invitation to honor rather than fear the rules because the rules are signposts directing us to Jesus. They are an invitation for us to step out of the rat race and onto the platform of Christ's declaration that we are good enough. They are an invitation for us to quit looking for perfect where it will never be found and to lose ourselves in the wonder of holy.

More than anything else, they're the belief that we have already been given what we've been searching for all this time.

Part One

Learning the Rules

CHAPTER 1

Longing for Home Runs

I have discovered that the realities of adulthood are more confusing than the questions of childhood ever were. For children, there are older, (hopefully) wiser people in our lives to direct the traffic of ideas that, without proper guidance, would drive us into dangerous situations (such as leaping from a twelve-foot jungle gym onto a trampoline and into a very shallow above-ground pool). When I was a kid, adults had one primary role to play, and more often than not they played it well: to make the rules. And I was a champion rule follower, jungle gym notwithstanding.

For me, rules were easy to follow. I was privileged to be raised by loving parents who worked hard to make sure my siblings and I could enjoy being kids. Life got pretty nuts in middle school when my mom and dad divorced, but still I enjoyed the simplicity of a well-ordered life. Right and wrong were black and white, and because I loved my parents so much I longed to please them and succeeded in all the ways that mattered to my Southern, Christian culture (for girls, anyway): I was always home by curfew, I didn't have sex, I didn't drink or smoke, I made good grades, and I had pretty responsible friends. If I stepped outside the boundaries laid down by my parents, I experienced swift and thorough consequences. It didn't take much to keep me in line.

Following the rules seemed as if it would get me pretty much anywhere I needed to go in life, and for a long time it did.

Until suddenly it didn't anymore.

What we learn as we grow up, as we're being shaped and conformed to standards set by those who came before us, is that life doesn't go by these rules. Tragedy doesn't listen to guidelines. Pain and suffering do not see our road signs and say, "Oops, let's turn around and go back!" The world operates on an axis completely out of our control, and so does every other person we meet. In fact, sometimes we wake up and discover that we are the ones we can't control. The rules no longer apply because the rules no longer make sense. The life we were living has shifted—perhaps it has been shifting for years without our notice—and like a ship whose navigation has been altered by a single degree, we have ended up somewhere we did not intend. At this point, we have to relearn the rules or toss them out completely in order to survive another day.

For me, there was so much shame in this discovery. I thought it was God I had been relying on for direction and purpose. In reality, it was the rules and not God in which my identity was found. When the rules stopped working in my favor, I assumed my identity was also lost, that it had vanished along with the value I believed my adherence to them had given me.

If this sounds familiar to you, we would probably be good friends. For the better part of a decade, I stumbled around in the dark looking for a new light to follow, a new set of rules that would once again order my life in a way that made sense. I don't know whether it will take ten years for you or if, perhaps, your being here will abbreviate the journey. But I do know that there is only so long you can avoid what your own body, your spirit, or God is trying to teach you. Sometimes the lesson comes over time, slow and steady, and sometimes it smashes into you with hurricane force. Either way, the challenge of accepting and applying the lesson falls on us. I pray with fervor for a change in the way we think about the rules, but it took a confrontation with my own long-hidden fears about failure in order for me to even see that a change was necessary. This book is the place where I lay down my need at the foot of the cross and ask you to join me, because it is there, and only there, where we will experience the sought-after transformation we hope to find on our Pinterest boards and Instagram feeds.

Growing up, I was a strong and solid softball player. Strong and solid are the words I'd use to describe most of what I've accomplished in life. I am never superb or number one or insanely, outrageously talented. I am strong and solid. Reliable. Counted upon. I am neither forgetful nor memorable, but somewhere in between. Above average, I suppose. I will not lie and tell you I've been satisfied with this outcome. All I ever wanted as a kid was to be the best at something. To impress. To get people clapping on their feet because of the awesomeness with which I succeeded. Succeeding was not satisfactory enough. I wanted to *exceed*. But on the softball field, as in many other cases, I was simply strong and solid.

I will never forget the first time I hit a home run. I was ten years old and towered over every boy in my grade. My dad—muscular and athletic and very, very patient with me—and my mother—a veritable beast on the softball field—had taught me everything I needed to know about how to hit well. I'd discovered the trick to hitting the ball where I wanted it to go, but while I was confident in my skills at that point, three years of playing recreational softball against the best players in my age group without ever hitting a home run had left me with the bitter taste of jealousy and day-old Big League Chew in my mouth. The time had come for me to show them what I was worth.

It was my last at-bat for that game and our team was ahead. I stepped up to the plate, adjusted my too-large helmet, and took my stance with the swagger of a ten-year-old who has a gaggle of teammates screaming her name at various decibel levels. When the pitcher tossed the ball, I stepped forward and swung the bat a half second earlier than normal. This technique ensured what my dad called a "sweet spot" impact, where the ball pinged beautifully off the near end of the bat and went soaring into left field. It whizzed past both the pitcher's head and the left center's glove and bounced just inside the fence. My skinny horse legs took me well past first base before the outfielders could even reach the ball and by then everyone on my team was screaming so wildly I felt like Benny "the Jet" Rodriguez. My coach, and best friend's father, was at third base swinging his arm around in circles and shouting at the top of his lungs for me to keep going. When I rounded third base, I locked eyes with my dad, who had started running from the dugout to meet me at home base. As soon as my foot hit the plate, he scooped me up onto his shoulders and bellowed, "That's my girl!" as the rest of my teammates banged on the dugout fence and ran to hug my legs.

Sometimes we get lucky enough to have a moment like this: a moment that seems to hover in midair, untouchable and pure. It dazzles like a Disney movie and becomes permanently etched on our minds as the standard to which all other moments should conform.

But my Hollywood-style home run was never repeated, even though I remained the strong and solid player I had always been. This was a constant source of frustration for my preteen self, and I gave up on softball when I tired of constantly missing the made-up mark. I moved on to other things, like music and cheerleading and track, and experienced the same frustration with them. I was smart. I could do a back handspring. I was a surprisingly skilled high jumper. I had an array of midlevel talents that served me well but never took me anywhere I thought worth mentioning for too long. In short, I wasted a lot of time and energy not enjoying my success because I was so occupied by my perceived lack.

I hit a lot of doubles and triples, but all I wanted was home runs.

At first glance, the rules seem simple enough. The church does a pretty good job of fitting stuff into boxes, even when it wasn't designed to fit, and we often begin our faith walk with what feels like a firm grasp on all that's expected of us. We cut out the obviously yucky stuff like too much alcohol or sex with people who don't care about us and attend church on a regular basis. We volunteer and make new friends and join a small group. We hit some home runs. Maybe we hit lots of them. But somewhere along the way we come face-to-face with the reality that what seems easy is really just new and exciting. The bright hope of transformation begins to wane and we look at the people who surround us and think, "Am I the only one who's struggling?"

We fall victim to our sin and stumble back into patterns of behavior that harm us. We realize that the joy of knowing Jesus doesn't eliminate suffering. We find ourselves thinking, like the apostle Paul, "I do not understand what I do. For what I want to do I do not do, but what I hate I do" (Rom. 7:15).

I have a friend from college whose love for Jesus is so evident that it seems to circle her body with light, and for a long time I envied her to the point that it was like an ache. I had been a Christian since childhood and there was much to be grateful for in my life, but she appeared to be on a whole other level in her relationship with the Lord and I was desperate for what she appeared to have.

I was missing something, only I wasn't sure what it was at the time. I had wonderful friends, a school I loved, strong family support, and a clear conscience. I was doing everything right as I had been taught to perceive rightness. So where did this longing come from? Why did I still feel as if it would never be enough?

Later, when I began to confront how the rules had influenced my view of God, I understood that trying to follow them without fail had exhausted me and some of the people I loved most. My relationship with my boyfriend had become incredibly strained because I refused to leave my expectations about faith at the door and because he seemed to want few expectations at all. I used rules about sex and church and theology to set up rigid and unforgiving boundaries for us, and he understandably resented it. That was the start of a new season for me, a season of questioning the rules that had been presented to me from birth and learning that there was something far richer to be experienced on the other side.

Before we go further, let me be clear: I believe that rules matter. Rules are guides to point us toward home to the God who saved us. They are not the beginning and the end of our faith, however, and they never should be. The rules are important to our understanding of history. They are necessary for contemplative study of Scripture, for prayer, and for personal growth. The rules are vital to our understanding of the King . . . but they are not the King.

Jesus lived the rules perfectly because we, as his children, are unable to earn our way, and also because he wanted us to see him— to seek him—above all things. Even the rules that have so often worked well in our favor. Then Jesus offered the Holy Spirit to us as the primary source for our righteousness. It is from the power of the Spirit *we already possess* that we are able to live out obedience. It is from the power of the Spirit that the fruit we long to see in our lives flourishes. It is not from obedience to the law alone. How can we even begin to keep the law without the Spirit of the only Person who ever accomplished it perfectly?

In her book *The Heart of Perfection*, Colleen Carroll Campbell wrote, "Letting go of perfectionism frees us to pursue real holiness instead of its self-righteous counterfeit." This letting go is both a collective and an individual necessity for us to thrive in faith, stewardship, and love. I realize this is a long, hard road. It is a conversation that gets to the very heart of what we believe about the rules and why.

I also realize that rules vary from person to person, from community to community. If I were to poll every person reading this book, we would not come away with the same answers about what is right and what is wrong. There are deep divides in the church, and that comes as no surprise to anyone. But I can almost guarantee every one of us would have intensely personal reasons about our beliefs. This is one rule that took me decades to learn. My assumption was that people who disagreed with me just had their theology wrong and needed to be convinced otherwise. I didn't understand that every one of us comes to faith with a history, even as children, and that such history is a cornucopia of families and stories, victories, and losses. We are complex and bursting with life even in the womb, and the thoughtfulness with which the Creator designed us is astounding. Why then do we so often ignore this complexity? Why do we approach another's difference in faith as though it is a threat to our own? Why do we count our own doubt as a strike against us when, in fact, almost nothing will grow us closer to Christ than the honest questions of the imperfect faithful?

I am not certain of many things, but I am quite sure the answer to these questions is fear. I have spent my life being afraid of too many unknowns. The rules I was given as a child helped me find my way through many of those fears. They gave me a map with a clear course charted to my ultimate destination, which, of course, was Perfection. I followed them with confidence and earnestness, and they produced many a wonderful thing in my life. But they did not produce holiness, and holiness was what I needed.

I still love rules. You'd think, because of what I've experienced, and as a creative person, that I would balk at rules altogether. No way. There's a reason why some of the most beautiful art is produced by people who excelled first in technique and then went their own more creative and more fulfilling ways. Breaking the rules is a successful tactic only if you know what they are and how they work.

So does God want us to defy him? No. But does God want us to trust him above all the things we think we know? Yes. Does God want us to submit to his leading despite our feeling we have all the right answers? Take a look at how Jesus responded to people throughout history—kings and military leaders, ordinary women and fisherman alike—and I think you'll find the answer is yes.

Years after my first home run, I still smile when I think of how my father taught me to hit that ball. I accomplished a goal I'd been trying to meet for years, and learning when to swing had equipped me for success. It was my dad's guidance that had showed me I needed direction to begin with, and without his voice speaking directly to my need, I would have never known what I was missing.

We are a generation in dire need of the Spirit. We have people raging about the rules of faith and putting people in tidy little categories so they don't have to do the hard work of actually listening to God. Because that's what a relationship is: work. It gets messy and hard, and no matter how many beautiful photos we see on social media of Bibles surrounded by candles and coffee, real transformation is more than showcasing our faith through a filtered photo. Real transformation is painful. Perfection can be faked, but holiness requires something of us.

And, let me assure you, that "something" is not that we make all the right choices.

It's not that we follow every rule by the book.

It's just *us*.

It's just you and me.

Because when we look at a God who created a world teeming with life and beauty and still saw fit to create humankind—and not just create us but call us his *best* creation—what is the purpose of holiness if there is never anyone to receive it?

CHAPTER 2

Problems with Purity

I was seven when I first learned to hate myself.
I had kept a secret that was so big and so heavy, it simply could not be carried for another second on the strength of my bony shoulders alone. It had to be put down. So one night, when I was nine I dropped it, quite mercilessly, on my older sister as she was trying to sleep across the room from where I sat on my bed, paralyzed by the thoughts racing through my mind. I couldn't move for fear of speaking the truth, for fear of what it would mean about me, and I couldn't keep my mouth shut for fear of keeping the ugly stuff inside. The words came tumbling out like a basket of kittens knocked on its side, except not as precious:

"Um, Beth?" I whispered, my voice shaking. "I have to tell you something."

"What?" she mumbled from her bed.

I swallowed hard. "Well . . . a couple of years ago my friend touched me. Down there."

Beth catapulted from her bed. "We have to go tell Mom and Dad," she said, pulling me toward the living room where our parents were still up watching television.

My mother had told me about sex when I was five, after my older sister ratted on me for boasting to my friend—with Barbie dolls as examples—that I knew babies started in the daddy and somehow ended up in the mommy. The logistics were way off, so while I'm sure it wasn't my sister's intention for me to receive an education on the subject, that's exactly what I got. My mom asked me at the kitchen island if I wanted to know what sex was, and I made the grave mistake of saying, "Sure." I had no idea what I was agreeing to.

After I learned what parts went where and how (I was still a little unsure about the why because, seriously, WHO WOULD DO THAT?), I asked more questions. My parents covered the emotional and spiritual aspects of sex and intimacy and then somehow skipped over the part about how I would soon start feeling things that made me want to touch and be touched in places I now knew were completely off-limits. As open as they were about the topic, I don't recall either one bringing up the subject of masturbation or boundaries on touching with friends. I think it was just assumed that because I had learned my genitals were for having sex and making babies—these were things I wouldn't be doing until I was good and married—the matter was closed.

But then I made a new friend, and her name was Julia.

Julia was an only child whose house made our three-bedroom ranch look like a palace. She was growing up poor in a small town filled with old money, and I pitied her. Our friendship felt more like an obligation than anything else, and I was never fully comfortable at her house, where evidence of emotional and physical neglect was apparent. I could see right away that even though my parents shopped for our clothes at Walmart and name brands were rare in our home, Julia was living at a level of poverty my seven-year-old brain could not compute. I couldn't reconcile my loving, comfortable home with what I saw at Julia's house. Being there made me feel out of sorts, as though her world was a more dangerous place simply because it was not as clean or as warm as mine.

I never wanted to be her friend. She was a nice girl, but every time we were together she invited me to come on some sort of rebellious adventure that, tempted as I was to misbehave, caused a gnawing twist in my stomach. I let my guard down with her and accepted things I would have refused to anyone else. I lived in constant discomfort. It didn't occur to me until later in life that Julia might have felt as uncomfortable as I often did. Perhaps she thought making friends meant acting out, the way I thought being kind meant giving in.

One night at Julia's house, her parents watched a movie we weren't allowed to see. I recall a glimpse of a scene that was too risqué for a pair of seven-year-olds and, later, after we were supposed to be in bed, the movie got brought up in conversation. While I can't even remember what was said, suddenly an idea as discomforting as it was tempting was floating in the air between us. We knew that what adults did with their bodies was not meant for us, but why the heck was it so intriguing? And why did it make me want to hide my face in shame and run to the bathroom for a bit of privacy?

I was curious about the physical stuff I had seen on television, despite my parents' protective guidance, and felt shame about this curiosity because I knew, in theory, about sexual intimacy and how it was intended to be enjoyed. But I was seven, with a frontal lobe still in its early stages of development, and I didn't know how to stop what was happening. Months of saying yes to Julia when I wanted to say no, of trying to fill in relational gaps in her life, muted the voice that told me to speak up and call my parents. When Julia decided to seek some answers to her questions, in a moment that was so brief I can only recall a few snapshots, I allowed and even invited it. Dressed in our nightgowns, she got on top of me. I gave her permission to put her hand between my legs, and she pressed her palm flat against my body, then removed it just as quickly. It was over so fast, but in that instant my little heart filled with a sense of worthlessness that was so overwhelming I wanted to die of shame. Julia moved on to other topics within minutes, questions forgotten, but I rolled over to face the wall, at war with myself, while she talked on and on about how we should try to stay awake all night.

Sadly, those few seconds would become the filter through which I'd view sexuality, and my own worth, for years and years to come.

I cried to myself a few different times that night as I stared at the wall of Julia's bedroom. As it turned out, we did end up staying awake all night long—reading books, talking, and trying to keep our eyes from closing—and when my dad picked me up the next day I moved like a zombie from both exhaustion and anxiety. My mind could not accept a reality where mine and Julia's behavior was typical or acceptable. I felt certain, as I stepped out of the car and into our house, that my parents would despise me if they ever knew what had happened.

It was the very first lie I ever believed.

For two years, I didn't talk about that night with anyone, even Julia. I carried it with me and saw its shadow rush in over every happy moment, like a specter beckoning me to remember what I really was: a perverse failure to my parents, incapable of ever being forgiven.

That was the second lie I believed, that curiosity about my body and Julia's interest in exploring her feelings with me were sins that deserved damnation. They weren't sins at all, but developmentally normal adolescent behavior. This is the problem with a lot of our talk about purity, whether implicit or explicit, in the church.

When we think of evil, we don't often think of it in relation to children, unless children are the victims. We imagine that Satan goes after adults and children are simply lost in the cross-fire. I don't want to stoke fear, but I believe it's important to face truth. Our enemy is as real and as active in the lives of our little ones as he is anywhere else in the world, and he celebrates when he does damage to the psyche of a young child, especially when that damage is done to how she views her sexuality. Sex is a sacred expression of unity, and it was given to us by a good God who wanted his children to experience intimacy with him in a tangible way. If our view of sex can be perverted, then unity with each other—and with God—becomes that much more difficult.

Julia's and my behavior is common for most children, and it's part of developing a healthy sexuality when shared with trusted adults who are willing both to set boundaries and to discuss them freely without shame or judgment. It makes people uncomfortable to talk about, I know, but stories like these are common for many people. When they get buried, they cause trauma that could have been avoided if we had felt able to talk about them.

I had other innocent experiences with friends, but Julia was the only one with whom I didn't feel safe or known, so I turned my anger at myself into resentment toward her and eventually refused to offer my friendship altogether. I told a few people about what had happened between me and Julia, but I was scared to tell the truth that I had been just as curious, that I had allowed all of it to happen because I felt I had no other choice. Nor did I share that fact with my parents, who put a stop to my friendship with Julia and kept her from me as best they could, which only served to increase my guilt because I had said yes, too, and she had never even known I was uncomfortable. Their response was valid. They had been terrified Julia was actually a cover-up for something—and someone—more sinister, especially when, trembling with tears, I asked them, "Am I still a virgin?"

For a couple of years, I was unkind to Julia in the way that elementary-aged children often are not kind. She apologized for the situation and I let her, but I was too ashamed to apologize for my cool behavior in return. I dismissed her efforts to remain friends and once wrote her a note saying she wasn't cool enough to hang out with me anymore. It was the one time in my life when I can remember actively trying to hurt another person. By the time we were teens, the whole mess seemed as if it had never happened, but it was always there in my mind, hidden beneath the surface. Julia was a reminder of what I viewed as a massive moral failure on my part. While my heart was tender toward the difficulties she faced in life, the quiet but powerful voice that told me I was wrong and unlovable kept me from reaching out in more than just superficial ways.

I go back to the night I told my parents about Julia, the night I asked them about the state of my virginity, and I want to cry for my childhood self. To think that I already viewed my worth as a person through the lens of my sexuality is as frustrating as it is hurtful. My concerns over what would happen to me if I didn't make all the right decisions about sexuality from then on ruled every romantic relationship I had in high school and college. Sometimes they even ruled my friendships. I became adept at creating rigid boundaries for myself and cried in disbelief when I'd discover that my friends had different sets of rules. Purity, the way I learned it, was my goal, and I had a hard time understanding why others weren't on board.

Its heyday was in the nineties, but the purity movement is still very much alive. Women are the ones most likely to grapple with the consequences of its teachings. It is our bodies that are sexualized time and time again. We are the ones who are held to a higher standard, who get cast aside, snubbed, or forgotten, unless of course our sexuality needs to be used as a lesson on the need for modesty.

Purity is a much broader concept than just not having sex before marriage. It has more to do with the culture and the environments that fuel our thinking—and, therefore, our actions—than it does with hemlines, one-piece bathing suits, and white wedding dresses. (These were all strictly enforced in my childhood faith, as if guidelines for such things were to be found directly in the New Testament Gospels.) The moment our cultural interpretations of purity come at the cost of our ability to connect with others, our feelings of value and self-worth, our very belief in God—then they have failed. They have become something more insidious. They have become an idol.

In her book *Shameless*, author and pastor Nadia Bolz-Weber writes, "Our purity systems, even those established with the best of intentions, do not make us holy. They only create insiders and outsiders. They are mechanisms for delivering our drug of choice: self-righteousness, as juice from the fruit of the tree of knowledge of good and evil runs down our chins." She goes on to offer a clear distinction between purity and holiness as we have traditionally understood them in American evangelical culture. "Purity most often leads to pride or despair, not to holiness. Because holiness is about union with, and purity is about separation from."

Our pursuit of purity is not the problem; it's the execution of the pursuit. It's the purpose behind the pursuit. What was I, as a young woman, hoping to accomplish by keeping my clothes on? Was it the desire to be more like the Savior I knew and loved? Or was it the pride of achieving—or maintaining—something valued so highly in the church that it had become another god to worship?

I didn't feel comfortable going to my parents with questions about my body, because I was already well-versed in fear, so I allowed my questions to be poorly answered by a friend. I don't blame my mom and dad for this chain of events, because they were simply trying to protect me. They did what parents are supposed to do. No one could have known how that moment with Julia would impact me in the years to come.

Shame directed my decisions and my view of God to a place from which I'm still trying to find my way back. Perfection was all I cared about once upon a time. Perfect behavior, perfect beliefs, perfect purity. (What even is that?) I wasn't aware, then, as Bolz-Weber wrote, that there was a distinction between these things and holiness.

I didn't understand, then, that in Christ I had already been made perfect, so any extra effort on my part was like spitting into the wind. Holiness was the longing of my heart and my body, but the filter I used to see the world, the one that had me performing for accolades on high alert for any perceived threat to my goodness—purity—damaged my vision.

There should be more to the Christian life than the pursuit of righteousness, because righteousness is a fruit of the Spirit. It is the result of something else, something far greater than receiving affirmation for our right deeds. We were never meant to settle for mere acceptance, and we were never meant to be put up on pedestals, whether we built them on our own or found ourselves shoved atop them by others.

In *The Four Loves*, C. S. Lewis writes that there are two types of nearness to God. The first is nearness in our relationship, what we do to position ourselves before the Father each day. This is essentially how close we are to God and how much time and energy we spend on what builds our intimacy with him, such as prayer, reading and studying Scripture, worship, serving, and fasting. The second is nearness in likeness. Likeness, Lewis notes, is altogether more sturdy because it is fixed. Finished. Unchangeable. It is an identity stamped upon us from the moment of our conception and it cannot be altered, regardless of our choices. I didn't know this at seven years old.

You see, you cannot change your identity as an image-bearer of God. You can love the Father, despise him, or doubt his existence completely, but you cannot unbecome who you are. If you are a Jesus follower, you can neither earn nor un-earn your salvation.

If you were a child like me, a girl who was dearly loved and still carried a hidden fear that everything I believed about that love was built on sand, let me assure you that the devil is a liar and the truth is not in him. The first question he ever asked humans was this zinger he poised to Eve in the Garden of Eden:

"Did God really say . . . ?"

That's the question that has been uprooting lives ever since.

Still, when the Lord went walking through the garden later that day, knowing good and dang well that Adam and Eve had chosen to disobey him and were hiding, what did he do? God asked where they were. I believe he also asked me this question that night at Julia's house as I turned to face the wall and cried. I picture the clench of God's heart for the pain he saw in mine and consider the anger he must have felt about what innocence I had lost. Not because I had sinned, but because the enemy had tricked me into believing the voice I heard, that whisper of condemnation, belonged to my heavenly Father.

As with Adam and Eve, God offered me an open line of communication. We serve a gracious and just Father, who made up his mind about us a long time ago, long before we misunderstood his directives about purity and took it upon ourselves to shame and berate one another for daring to make mistakes. Whether the circumstances you find yourself in right now are a result of your own sins or someone else's (or a convoluted combination of the two), the way forward is into the open arms of a Creator who will never call you anything but his. He will never call you anything less than pure, than good, than holy.

I want you to learn to run full tilt to the voice that comforts and leave the lies behind. Embrace your likeness, my friend. It's not going anywhere.

CHAPTER *3*

What Women Know

Your womanhood is a mighty thing.

I want to be sure you know that.

I recently sat in the family room of a friend while she and her husband debated the sex of their new baby, still nestled in utero. At one point, her husband declared his undying hope for a boy.

"We've gotta have a preacher in the family."

I laughed and countered, "Well, your daughter can always do that too."

Kindly, but firmly, he replied, "Not according to my theology."

Prior to this conversation, I had forgotten there were people who still believe women are unauthorized to lead in church. Not so long ago, I had shared their conviction.

The rules about women in leadership hadn't actually been an issue for me during adolescence. My family were members of a contemporary charismatic church. Besides our pastor getting up on stage what felt like every other month to tell us his wife was pregnant again, I hadn't noticed any particular view on the subject of a woman's role in church. With the exception of people speaking in tongues and laying hands on each other, all seemed quite proper and undramatic to a young me.

My dad, a staunch conservative who harbored a disdain for the word *feminist*, never once made me feel like I couldn't do something because I was a girl. He loved me as all fathers should love their daughters, and I thrived under his tender care. My father taught me so much about life, about how to steward my gifts, and I loved learning from him. Some of my favorite memories of us together are of his teaching me how to care for my first car, which was a black 1987 Chevrolet Camaro in basically mint condition. Every weekend I spent at his house included some time underneath the hood of that American muscle, learning how to change the oil or replace a belt, and I reveled in it. I loved the throaty power of the engine and the way I felt climbing out of it on a warm summer evening. I was not a girl afraid of being seen, and because of that confidence I was unafraid of what being seen meant.

One fall semester in college, I signed on to help lead worship at a nearby newly planted Baptist church, which was holding services in a tiny conference room of the local community center. A few weeks into my tenure there, the church leadership took me and a handful of other volunteers out to eat for steaks with a side of why they believed women were not fit to serve as pastors or lead men. This was their attempt to lay out a full explanation of the church's view on major issues before we jumped on board as members. We ate in a private room at the restaurant so they could show us a PowerPoint presentation, and I listened and enjoyed my steak without too much mental strife. Their exegesis of Scripture was rote and familiar, and when I felt an internal bristling, I dismissed it as selfish pride. These were the rules and I must learn to obey them.

I stayed on with the church for a few more weeks and, for reasons I couldn't then articulate, never returned after Christmas break. I learned two years later, when I walked into a Presbyterian church on the other side of town and saw our former music minister there greeting congregants at the door, that the church had closed less than a year after that steak dinner. When I inquired about why, he grimaced and said, "It just wasn't good." I stepped into the Presbyterian church that morning with a strangely justified disposition. My instincts had been right, but I still had no idea what those instincts had protected me from.

There are many difficult circumstances in life that I have not had to face. I will never know what abuses I have been spared because of the privileges I've been afforded or because of the sheer luck of walking away before it got bad. What trauma I have faced, while painful and challenging to overcome, has been softened by my status as a straight, white, cisgender person. These are the categories still most likely to garner access where others are denied. I never knew about my own privilege because I didn't have to; I could walk through life in many ways unscathed. While my womanhood is a testy subject within the church, a queer woman of color is going to face even greater difficulty being seen and heard, if at all in some cases. This is a shameful and unfortunate reality among believers, and we still have a whole lot of work to do.

The last few years have been exceptionally troublesome for women in ministry. Popular bloggers and speakers who have done powerful and important work for the kingdom have been called out for a lack of accountability. There are complaints about many of these female teachers having never attended seminary, but it does not seem to faze some that a number of influential Christian men have the same, or even fewer, qualifications. Women who have been planting and leading ministries for twenty years or more, women who have led the charge in bringing justice to marginalized groups and risked their reputations for the sake of his glory, are nevertheless labeled inadequate. I cannot help looking at the primary difference between these two groups of leaders and come to the conclusion that it is not qualifications we require, but a particular set of genitalia. This is the state of our union, is it not?

Women are gifted and strong and created in the image of God. We know that we were created with purpose. What we question is how these gifts and how these strengths are meant to be used. Where do the answers come from? Should we rely solely on the leadership of the church to provide them, as those men in the steakhouse believed we should, or do we turn to our own interpretations of Scripture? That leads to a rabbit trail of other questions we will never fully agree on how to answer, but here's our common ground: women, too, are endowed with the power of the Holy Spirit, whom Jesus sent to be our Helper and who inhabits the innermost place of every believer.

As authors I admire, such as Sarah Bessey and the late Rachel Held Evans, have taught me, women and men are equally called to bear, and to be, the Good News. Women are not minor players in the kingdom of God, necessary only for the raising up of children and other women. We are essential to all God's good works.

I actually think my father raised me to be a feminist (but don't tell him I said so). We've spent so many hours of my life discussing the intersection of politics and religion, and while a gracious plenty of my beliefs have changed since I was a young adult, one thing that hasn't is an unalterable certainty in the value of womanhood. No matter how you present yourself, whether you subscribe to traditional notions of femininity, eye them with suspicion, or think they should be abolished, your womanhood is an inherently powerful thing. It is not to be feared or diminished; it is to be celebrated and honored.

It was through a woman's body that Jesus entered the world, that he became incarnate and present with us. And it was through the power of the Holy Spirit, his helper, that every believer is transformed into the fullness of Christ. In both Hebrew and in Aramaic, the language of Jesus, the word for Holy Spirit is a feminine noun. I don't think it's a coincidence that women share this name with the Wisdom of God. We are vessels of wisdom for our friends, our coworkers, our children, our spouses, our families, our nation. We lead, teach, and nourish the people around us with our words, and we receive this nourishment in return in the form of healthy communities. Without women, none of this works.

The Trinity, which represents both male and female aspects of God, is unified, the kind of unity we, as their children, were intended to share. I wish this unity could be fulfilled in our lifetime, but we have already been assured that the world offers no lasting hope in the way of justice and redemption. That is a job for our Savior alone. I don't mean to imply that we stop standing against injustice or working to use our privilege for the sake of others, only that the work will not stop until Christ has come to take us home. I look forward to that day. I long for a world as beautiful as this one but where all that's wrong has been made right: where everything confusing or desperate or gut-wrenchingly awful has been redeemed to glory. It was C. S. Lewis, in his book *Miracles*, who said, "Redeemed humanity is to be something more glorious than unfallen humanity."

In the meantime, while we live on this imperfect planet, Christ invites us to delight in what he has already redeemed: us. His children. His daughters. As surely as we can declare Christ our Savior, we can declare his holiness ours. Despite what I've heard, I am not less than. I am not my thoughts or my fears or my uncertainties. I am not what the world says I am. My identity is found in Jesus Christ, the Lamb of God. I am my beloved's and my beloved is mine.

I think of the women who knew Jesus when he walked on earth and wonder what it must have been like for them to hear, probably for the first time, that their lives had value and meaning beyond what humankind had deemed appropriate. That they were essential to the kingdom of God. That they were seen and known and loved and powerful. Imagine hearing those words directly from the lips of our Savior. I can tell you they remain true of us, as well, regardless of what any pastor or family member or internet troll has to say about it. Jesus's words live on in Scripture, and they belong to us now even as they belonged to the women Jesus knew then.

God is not waiting for us to be perfect women, perfect mothers, or perfect leaders. God is not holding his love just out of our grasp, teasing us with what we can never truly call our own. He is as near to you as your very breath and he is whispering, "Good. Holy. Beloved. Called." The world demands that we earn these titles. Jesus invites us to claim them, and it's in the claiming that we discover how to live them.

4

Losing Our Fear

Becoming a mother has meant learning to face all the things I do not know, even when I think I do.

(Which is often: tell me you've noticed.)

Just like her mother, my daughter, Lucy, is a chatterbox. She has a lot of words. She loves to ask all manner of random questions, ranging from such topics as jungle animals and tornadoes to local species of birds and why Columbus was "not a nice guy." Also like her mother, Lucy has limits to her curiosity.

As we were driving home after school one day, Lucy began telling me her own silly version of a ghost story. It was the week before Halloween and I had told her I was reading one of my favorite book series, a five-part ghost story about a Charleston realtor who can see and communicate with the dead. I'm not into horror, but I like to get a little creeped out. Lucy took my admission as an invitation to start talking in her spooky voice—which has a British accent for some reason—and what followed was a hilarious and wonderful ghost story in which she used the phrase "On a dark and stormy night." Besides being impressed with my five-year-old's talent for creating atmosphere with her words, I was tickled to death. Then my mama brain turned on and I started wondering what kind of effect our discussion of ghosts was going to have on her little mind.

I was not allowed to celebrate Halloween as a kid. Instead, every year we attended our church's annual Hallelujah party. It included all the stuff we've come to associate with this holiday in America—hayrides, costumes, pumpkins, and tons of candy—without any of the dead-coming-back-to-life stuff. (Funny, because Christians are normally really big on that kind of thing.) I didn't go trick-or-treating for the first time until I was eleven, and then only because I prepared a whole report about the Christian origins of Halloween and presented it to my dad with the seriousness of a marketing executive hoping to land a huge client. I didn't miss out on anything important growing up, but I want to give my kid the chance to safely run amok with her peers while also keeping her experiences age appropriate.

As I clarified to Lucy that ghosts were not real and that all the monsters we see on Halloween cannot actually hurt us, I soon spiraled into a monologue that ended with my commentary on why evil exists in the world. Lucy waved her hands back and forth as I explained the complexities of free will and said, "Mom, stop! It's too much."

I pulled a face like my mother's and blinked rapidly at the realization that I had gone too far. My attempts to encourage and enlighten my child had frightened her instead, and while I backtracked in an effort to fix my mistake, the Holy Spirit called to my mind an old favorite: "For God has not given us a spirit of fear, but of power and of love and of a sound mind" (2 Tim. 1:7, NKJV).

Lucy's sensitivity to what I was saying is not a flaw in her character, but a strength. I'd like to think it is a strength she got from me, but I am often not wise enough to shake my head and say, "Stop! It's too much." I allow myself to get sucked into the world's troubles in a way that leaves me paralyzed rather than activated. I say yes when I need to say no. I give into the spirit of fear and lose the connection to God's power and all that comes with making room for him to rule in my heart.

My daughter possesses a childlike wisdom I can't seem to access anymore. I have lived a life marked by its limits—on my body, my passion, my experiences, my joy—out of fear that I would lose my very identity if those boundaries were not in place. I am curious at times how much healthier I would be if, instead, I had made those choices out of power, out of love, and from a sound mind.

This could be a game changer for those of us who believe in the value of the law but disagree with the voices who tell us it is for fear that Christ has set us free. Jesus lived, died, and rose again so that we could walk in the assurance of all that is available to us in him, both in heaven and on earth. He didn't live, die, and rise again so that we would forever remain shackled to our fear. If we are going to lose something, I don't want it to be our passion or our joy, but our tendency to cower rather than put our hands up and say, "Stop! This is too much."

Too much legalism. Too many lies about our neighbors and ourselves. Too much settling for the rules when we have been offered the love, the power, and the peace of the Ruler.

I long for a generation of people to fully embrace our gifts . . . and I also long for us to embrace our limits. We need to flip the script on what we've been told and what we still believe about putting up guardrails. We are limited. We are flawed. We are in desperate need. These things are evidence not of a lack of value but of a lack of authorship. They are indicators of being the created rather than the Creator. I don't look at my children and condemn them for their ignorance, and the God of the universe doesn't condemn us either. But he does want us to resist settling into our ignorance and acting as if he doesn't have more to offer. Let's hold up our hands and say, "Stop! It's too much!" to a world that tries to convince us it has all the answers.

That's a quick path to a lost and exhausted life, and the solution is not better behavior or more control, but submitted, transformed hearts.

I am grateful our culture is beginning to see that perfection is not the goal. Authenticity and vulnerability are huge buzzwords, and rightfully so, but I sometimes feel we have swung too far in the opposite direction. Forgoing all sense of responsibility in the name of being authentic is just as dissatisfying as stuffing ourselves with self-righteous pride. Any time I have found myself drifting to one of these extremes—and those times have been frequent—it doesn't take long before I am anxious and uneasy, on the search again for something that will settle my restless soul.

What would it look like for me to both accept my humanity and actively turn it over to the Lord? How can we be practical in losing our fear and finally gaining our lives?

●　•˙　●••　　●

I suffer from Obsessive Compulsive Disorder, also known as OCD. It is a symptom of my struggles with perfectionism.

"Not perfect, but extremely rare," reads a T-shirt I wear from time to time. It's a helpful reminder of what matters when my brain tries to keep me fixated on what is—or what could be—wrong in life. Buried deep beneath the obsessions and compulsions that keep me locked in a vicious cycle is the fear that found roots in the soil of my heart long before I knew it was there. The fear of being bad, wrong, or immoral, the fear that if I didn't police every single thought and action, then I would somehow lose complete control and become a vicious monster who murdered people for fun. That's extreme, I know, but it's the nature of OCD. It's the nature of growing up with a view of God where faithfulness means a performance worthy of a standing ovation in every situation. There is often no room in my mind for gray, for the middle space where most of life is lived out in its average, mundane acceptability. I am either perfect or entirely lost. It's exhausting.

This fear spread out far and wide, at home inside of me, and it sprouted above the soil when I became an adult. You might not suffer with OCD, but I can guarantee you have some powerful roots that have taken hold of something valuable in your life. You probably have some kind of fear that has stolen from you. And while you want to dig up those roots, the pain of exposing them feels like an even greater risk than living with them for the rest of your life. This is a pain I know intimately.

A phrase I have written down in my journal is one I repeat to myself again and again: "Feelings are not always truth-tellers, but they are always indicators." Fear, and our ability to feel it, is not always a lie, as the expression goes. God equipped us with amygdalae, and I quite appreciate a brain that alerts me to risk. Without it, I wouldn't survive very long, so the primary question is not whether our fear is lying to us but why we are feeling fear in the first place. An answer to the latter also answers the former and—BONUS!—helps us clear the path to a healthy reverence for things that can harm us without also crippling our faith.

In the book of Isaiah, God warns the prophet not to fall into the same mindset as the people of Judah, who were (understandably) frightened of the encroaching armies of Israel and Syria but had neglected to trust in God and, instead, had given their fear free reign to rule over their minds and hearts: "Don't be like this people, always afraid somebody is plotting against them. Don't fear what they fear.

Don't take on their worries. If you're going to worry, worry about The Holy. Fear God-of-the-Angel-Armies" (Isa. 8:12–13, MSG).

The word *fear* can also be translated "revere." God was asking Isaiah not to revere what the people of Judah revered. They were standing firm on the foundation of what scared them and, as humans are skilled at doing, had forgotten the God who had rescued them many times before. In the previous chapter of Isaiah, King Ahaz had been assured that Judah would not be overtaken by Israel and Syria, but his fear led him to bribe the Assyrians for protection and, eventually, they turned on Judah and caused incredible destruction.

What do these verses show us about the God-of-the-Angel-Armies? He is almighty. He is in control. He is holy. He can be trusted. He is fiercely protective of his children's hearts and will not stand idly by while we fill them up with what he has warned us against. God was not asking the people of Judah to disregard their emotions. He is the One who made them, after all. He was challenging them—as he is challenging us—not to let their emotions rule them.

In the end, Judah suffered extensive harm at the hands of the Assyrian army, but the capital city of Jerusalem was saved as a result of Isaiah's prophecy. This leads me to wonder how much else could have been saved if the citizens of Judah had heeded the call. How much could be saved in our lives if we would take captive the fear in our hearts to the God who is always with us?

A few verses later, in Isaiah 8:14, God tells the prophet he will be "a stone that causes people to stumble and a rock that makes them fall." And he remains a stumbling block even now to those of us who continue to be ruled by our fear. The way of Jesus is offensive to those who have built their homes on right theology and correct beliefs. We live in a divisive period of history, and the church is being called to account for its wrongs to the body, including members of the LGBTQ community, people of color, women, and victims of abuse. Fear does not lead to life and wholeness; fear leads to the idols of legalism and exclusivity. Fear leads us to reject those God calls his own because we are afraid of losing the approval of those in our circle of influence, and we tread on dangerous ground when we walk that path.

We regain so much commonality, as believers, when we revere what God reveres. Jesus declared that the love of God is his greatest commandment, and he followed it up with the command to love our neighbors along this stipulation: "as ourselves." How would I choose to be loved? With supernatural grace and mercy, with truth and good humor. This is the way Christ has loved me, and so it is what I long to experience from others. We are shaped for love, to receive it and to give it, and if we remove love from our theology, we are but "clanging cymbals." I don't want to put words in God's mouth, but there is no denying what he would give—and has given—for his children. It is our responsibility, as disciples of Jesus, to do the same.

When our fear of getting things wrong or losing the world's affection convinces us that rigid dogma or condemnation is the way to righteousness, we have chosen the lies of our enemy. We have failed to love even ourselves and we have shut off the power, love, and sound mind available to make us holy. We've rejected our gifts in favor of being right.

I long for us to choose the way of Jesus, who showed us the Father in real time, and trust that he is still with us, still revealing his majesty in every moment we submit to him. Just like my daughter, Lucy, who made her feelings known, as God's beloved children we get to decide if we want him to be our stumbling block as we choose perfection over people or the solid Rock upon which we stand.

CHAPTER 5

Sing the Song of Hope

Until the summer I turned twenty-two, perfectionism had always worked in my favor. If you made the right choices, you lived a happy life. It was that simple, and it had always been that reliable.

I had just graduated from Georgia Southern University with big dreams about the world that lay in front of me, and I hoped to move to Nashville and maybe try to get over my stage fright. I loved to write and sing, and I had spent my college years hoping against hope that one day I would stop quaking with fear every time I stepped on stage. Choral performances and musical theater were no problem. I loved them. But solo acts? They weren't for me, no matter how often I told myself that THIS would be the time I'd suddenly get it all together.

My freshman year, I auditioned to sing the national anthem at a basketball game, and while the audition went well, the performance was a total bust. I struggled to stay on pitch because I was shaking like a leaf until I dropped into a lower key so my voice wouldn't crack when I hit the high F at the end. That night, a guy I knew from marching band christened me "Key Change Girl." I was emotionally scarred and nicknamed, two things that don't go away easily.

I woke up the next morning with a pit in my stomach and a bright crimson flush on my cheeks. I had failed at the one thing I wanted to do well, and I had to perform the song again two weeks later. I practiced with a vocal coach—one of my professors at the university—and even though I still felt like I was going to throw up, my second performance was fine. Forgettable, but fine. For the rest of college, I never expressed interest in singing without also apologizing for it, as though my public failure meant I had no right to be there even though music was one of my biggest joys.

I wasn't classically trained like many of my peers. Music wasn't my major; it was my minor. But I could hear a melody and match pitch. I had also been reading music since I was ten. I would listen to the girls around me hitting notes I could only dream about and want to sink into the ground. In my mind, no one cared about altos. There would never be an audience member who gasped at the sound of my low C sharp. Everyone came for the notes that shattered glass. My average voice was useful in an ensemble, and perhaps it would have been above average if I had stuck with training and worked with my skill level instead of against it, but for a girl who had grown up equating perfection with worth, anything less than impressive was a waste. I kept forgetting how singing is as physical as any sport, and it requires practice to be good, even for those with ridiculous natural talent.

I didn't have a plan mapped out for how I would get to Nashville. I was naive and still working with the mindset that a high GPA and a degree would find me a job easily enough. That's what life looked like for me up until that point. Nothing thrilled me more than achievement and success, whether it was in class or in my everyday life, and so the prospect of moving to a city I had never even been to was exhilarating . . . despite the fact that I had made little effort to actually get there.

The truth was that deep down I knew music wasn't for me. I was simply trying to make myself fit, and the effort was like trying to turn cookie dough into a cookie without actually baking it: still somewhat enjoyable, sure, but not quite right. Anytime I would think about looking for a job, I would find something else to occupy my mind instead. There was always tomorrow.

That summer, I lived without worry. I babysat my nieces, a job I felt I could have done forever, and drove to see my now-husband, Pierce. We had been dating for a little less than a year, although our story went much further back than that, and things were pretty serious. He, along with almost all of our friends, was still at Georgia Southern that fall for one more year, and the idea of everyone going back to school without me was not nearly as disconcerting in May as it would become in July. I was under the impression that life would continue to go as it had always gone, and that, no matter what, I would continue to be as good at it as I had always been.

● · · ●●●   ·
●   ●

It was a bright Tuesday morning, and I woke up early when my mom came into my room to kiss me and my little sister goodbye as she left for work. Kati is eleven years younger than me, so ten years ago the difference in our age was stark: I was fresh out of college and she was about to start middle school. Being back at home had begun to feel less like a summer vacation and more like a prison sentence, and my sister helped keep me sane even while I spent most of my afternoons acting as her second mother. She and I were inseparable, both by proximity and choice, and it wasn't uncommon for Kati to fall asleep in my bed after a night spent watching movies or playing on my computer. I would wake up to the bright summer sun streaming through the windows, get dressed, make breakfast, and read while Kati did tweenager things. It was a peaceful season. But on that morning, when I was still bleary-eyed from sleep, my brain was a hive of activity. I'd had a dream that bothered me, as dreams can do when they feel so real you aren't sure what's true and what's not, and I couldn't stop thinking about it.

I took Kati to an afternoon summer camp and then went back to my mom's house by myself. She lives in a beautiful home at the end of a cul-de-sac, nestled in the trees far back from the road. The house is full of windows, and the front porch overlooks a creek that sounds like a sleep machine. It's a beautiful place, and quite serene. On that Tuesday, though, the isolation made me feel anxious, and being alone gave my mind nothing to do but chew on itself.

I remember the moment it happened with such clarity that, a decade later, I still experience the sharp twist in my gut and the chill of my mind on my skin. If you've ever had an intrusive thought, the kind of thought that stuns you with its horror, then you understand what happened to me. Intrusive thoughts are common, and we all have them at some point in our lives. Maybe you've visited the Grand Canyon and stood at the precipice, marveling at its size and depth, and suddenly found yourself wondering what it would be like to step off the edge. Or maybe you've chatted with your friend in the kitchen, and without warning the knife in your hand becomes a weapon with which you imagine stabbing your loved one. These thoughts are disturbing, but normal. Our brains make connections on their own without our effort all the time because we are constantly receiving input and stimulation that gets stored away and pulled out at random moments. For most people an experience like that makes you shake your head in bewilderment and then go on about your day.

Not me.

I know now that my thought didn't actually mean anything, but at the age of twenty-one my understanding of OCD was limited to the knowledge that there were some people in the world who had to wash their hands a hundred times a day. I knew nothing of triggers, or mindfulness, or the capacity for the brain to function independently of my choosing. I also didn't even know I had OCD then. All I knew was that I'd had a terrible, crippling thought—a thought I feared was based in reality because of my dream the night before—and it carried with it more meaning about my identity than any external evidence to the contrary.

I viewed my thought as evidence of something I had never noticed before, and it scared the hell out of me.

It is not an exaggeration to say that I spent the next twenty-four hours in a state of full-fledged terror. I was having what is clear to me now as my first panic attack. Because of the nature of this attack, the fact that my own thought was the catalyst, I assumed there was something deeply, inherently wrong with me and, thus, I couldn't bring myself to tell anyone about it for days.

I'm a compulsive confessor (I mean, HELLO, I'm writing a book about this stuff), and I have to talk about what I'm feeling or I'll get so emotionally tangled up I can hardly focus on anything for more than a few seconds. I told my mom about my dream and my intrusive thought, and as she is wont to do, she asked a few questions. She has advanced degrees in psychology and has worked with the cognitively disabled for twenty years, so she understands something about the mind. Her questions, which were similar to the ones I'd hear in my counselor's office eight years later, were meant to help me see reason and calm down. But my emotions were so acutely attuned to what was happening in my brain that reason and evidence were rendered useless.

For the next six months, I trained myself in the art of compulsive behavior. I quickly learned how to manipulate any situation to fit my needs, and I excelled in the composition of days so I could successfully avoid any environment that would trigger an episode. I knew that if I could avoid what made me so frightened of myself, then I wouldn't have to face it at all. If I didn't have to face it, I would never have to wonder about my identity or my self-worth. It was misery beyond description. I had never been so unhappy. I hadn't even thought such sadness was possible.

Until that Tuesday morning in July, almost every painful experience in my life had come from an external source, from someone else's poor judgment. I was the good girl, the girl who loved Jesus and made it her life's mission to get everything right no matter the circumstance. Mental illness was nothing more than a lack of faith, a lack of effort, from people who didn't understand that IF YOU JUST DO THIS, everything will be fine.

In response to other people's poor choices, I'd say things like:

"Just put the bottle down."

"Just keep your clothes on."

"Just stop doing that."

I had good intentions, but an obnoxious person with good intentions is still obnoxious. To top it off, I was still unemployed, and Nashville had long since become a joke I didn't tell anymore. The thought of moving away from the people I knew and loved was crippling, and I gave up on the idea of ever making a career in music. Not because I finally admitted it wasn't what I really wanted, but because I lost my hope. If I'm being honest, I gave up on virtually everything except just trying to get through another day.

I would sit on my purple love seat every night as the moon was rising and whisper tearful, urgent prayers to God to rescue me from this despair. I would confess my every thought to him and beg for forgiveness because what I had always believed about God's love was rooted in how well I played my part, just as my love of music had been dependent on how well I could actually perform it. I felt I had lost them both, and it ripped me apart in ways that make tears stream down my face as I write this.

In the months that passed after I flipped the tassel on my graduation cap, my life became a caricature of itself. The one obviously good thing that happened, which I clung to as my only source of hope for the future, was that on a spring-break trip to the Florida Keys with our college friends, Pierce asked me to marry him. The week prior to the trip, I'd spent a whole afternoon running through the list of intrusive thoughts I'd had since that morning in July, convincing myself that everything was okay, that thoughts weren't facts no matter how painfully they bruised. I also read Brennan Manning's *The Ragamuffin Gospel* and caught a glimpse of a God I had never truly known before, a God whose love remained unalterable in spite of my imperfections. In the book, the author details his struggle with alcohol abuse and the resulting loss of identity and self-worth. In the devastation that follows, he experiences the unmatched beauty of grace and discovers his equally unmatched inability to lose it. That sent a tiny glimmer of hope into my heart.

For two decades, perfection was the standard to which I had held myself. As with music, anything less than that felt like a waste. And it had taken me almost an entire year to step just one foot out of the endless shame cycle of dos and don'ts.

I suspect I'm not alone in this. We freeze ourselves in a season of loneliness or despair or fear and wake up one day to discover how much time has passed. Sometimes the desire for something better kicks us into a higher gear, but oftentimes we end up more depressed about our inability to save ourselves and just sink lower than we were before.

I am convinced that shame is Satan's greatest tool. It's not always obvious what he's doing the way we have been led to believe it is. He shows up with horns during war and violence, but even those things often begin with what looks a lot like goodness: a goal to achieve, a country to save, an injustice to right. Satan masquerades as something beautiful, something worthy, and when we believe what he says to us and act on it, he berates us endlessly for our mistake.

I fell for the lie that my worth was a conditional thing, and now I was hurting because of it. Suddenly, I had no choice but to hope the opposite was true—and that's really all I had: hope. I didn't feel in my heart what I had read about in Scripture or even seen lived out in life. Like so many women of faith, I scoured through the Bible searching for passages that would alleviate my suffering and ended up more at a loss than before. So much of what I heard at that time came from my own mind, from my own emotions, and I held on fast to the belief that if I didn't feel something, then it couldn't possibly be true.

Have you done that? Are you doing it now?

While our emotions are good and useful things, they are not always truth. They are not accurate guides for every decision or how valuable we really are. They are notes on a scale, moving up and down and back again. Low notes are not indications of a terrible life any more than they're an indication of a terrible composition.

They are simply a part of the song we're singing.

Part Two

Living the "Good" Life

CHAPTER 6

Love Can't Wait

If there's any life event that can lead to a perfectionist turning in upon herself, it's marriage. You say, "I do," and then you go home to a new partner, a new life, and a whole new set of expectations.

On that sunny November Saturday morning, I woke up exhilarated and exhausted. The night before, I had stayed up until 1:00 a.m. talking with one of my bridesmaids in my high school bedroom while a dozen of my closest friends slumbered in the house around us. I don't remember much of our conversation, but I do remember saying, "I can't believe that by this time tomorrow I'll be married." She joked, "I'm just excited that by this time tomorrow you won't be a virgin anymore."

My wedding to Pierce went like so many weddings do: a handful of our best-laid plans bombed, but the most important ones went off without a hitch. We married in a beautiful church neither one of us had ever attended. The day was full of laughter and happy tears. As Pierce's former youth pastor asked if he would have and hold me all the days of his life, Pierce crinkled his nose at me with a mischievous grin and gave a barely discernible shake of his head, like "Nah, just kidding." I laughed out loud. My family had long joked that I would never make it through our wedding without crying, since that is my modus operandi in times of great emotion, but my relationship with Pierce has been marked by humor and an extreme degree of silliness since the beginning. Our wedding would not be an exception. At the reception, we shoved cake in each other's faces and whispered jokes about how Pierce's lips got stuck to his teeth during the vows. Somewhere I have a sweet photo of my new mother-in-law caressing my face in what appears to be an affectionate gesture, but she was actually just trying to wipe a smear of blue icing from my cheek.

When it was all over, Pierce and I ran out of the church through a tunnel of bubbles and well wishes, eager to be finished with the pomp and circumstance. We piled into my car to leave, and I sent a cheeky grin to my friends, holding up my phone, making a show of turning it off before we left. After twenty-three years of holding out, I wasn't going to let anyone interrupt our first night together as husband and wife. In case of emergency, don't call me. Dial 911.

Ten minutes after we left the church, I realized I had forgotten my purse—and the birth control pills inside it—and we had to turn around and meet my parents at the previous exit to get it. As much as I adore my father, let me tell you how he was exactly the last person I wanted to see just before I rode off into the sunset to have sex with my husband for the first time. Awkward.

As a young evangelical, I had prepared for this moment. I was not one of those prudish types who left the room when people talked about sex. No, for years, I had listened with interest—and sometimes judgment—to all kinds of sordid and hilarious stories from my friends, and had been busy taking notes in my head about what sounded fun, sexy, or just plain gross about sex. I was full of confidence about what lay ahead—about the pleasure "guaranteed" to us by God because of our commitment to waiting for marriage—and felt no hesitation. I had even brought along the True Love Waits card I signed when I was thirteen to give to my husband when we arrived at the hotel. I was very precious, bless my heart, and despite all the harmless jokes made to the contrary, our first time together was all I had hoped it would be during my many years of waiting. For two days, we lived in a shiny bubble of eager, earnest romance—with room service and cheesy rom-coms—and we reveled in our new roles as husband and wife. Then we went home.

Forty-eight hours later, I woke up with a UTI. Then, a few hours after that, I had my first car accident. We spent all the money we'd been gifted at the wedding on my deductible, and I teased my husband that if this was what marriage was like, then I quit. The bubble had burst, and it was back to real life.

To top it all off, it took about three-and-a-half seconds before I understood that a wedding ring does not a flourishing sex life make. There are times when the connection is natural and effortless, and there are times when it takes work, communication, and an open mind. Sometimes, when life throws serious curveballs, it takes a generous glass of merlot.

The prevailing attitude from culture about the necessity of testing sexual compatibility with every partner ran contrary to my belief that sex was a covenant designed to flourish inside the boundaries of a healthy marriage. It still does. But the view that any sort of physical intimacy outside of marriage was sinful, along with the near silence on the subject from Christian culture unless the discussion was about what not to do, had not equipped me for the complexities of a sexual relationship with my spouse. I did not know that sometimes sex is awkward or frustrating or silly. I didn't know it could be full of fits and starts and still be pleasurable. I did not know that marriage would offer a plethora of sexual experiences—wonderful, terrible, and everything in between—and that both the church and the culture were a big, fat disappointment when it came to painting an accurate picture of what intimacy looks like between two very different people. In my mind, sex was primary in both marriage and the Christian life, another thing to get right in order to avoid eternal suffering. In reality, sex was so much more . . . and so much less.

Let's face it: we are obsessed with sex—obsessed with who is having it, who is not having it, how people are having it, and with whom. Despite our obsession, we refuse to lay all our cards on the table with honest discussions and, as a result, we have a generation of men and women who are now having sex and wrestling with why their experiences do not line up with what they were told—or not told—as adolescents. We have women who are passionate and adventurous but who struggled to flip the switch from "sex is bad" to "sex is good" when they walked down the aisle into real life with their partner. We have people enjoying sex with their spouses and feeling guilty about it because their brains didn't download the memo that, yeah, it's all good now. Old habits die hard. So does bad theology.

We have mistaken good behavior for guaranteed pleasure and bad behavior for misery, and now we are angry with God about the disconnect between the two. One chapter in a book won't change the way the world works, but a lot of chapters could start the conversation. There are authors and pastors more eloquent than myself, women in the church who are tired of the games we play, who are eager to move us in a healthier direction where sex is valued as a gift from the Lord and is at times—like all good gifts—an exercise in patience and humility. These are necessary conversations if we want our own intimate experiences to help us thrive and for our children to grow up with a more honest—and honorable—view of sex.

For many of us, sex feels a bit like spiritual whiplash. As we suspected when we were teenagers, it's really, really fun (nobody lied about that, at least), but we suppress our passionate emotions because we never learned to embrace them well. Our bodies and our spouses tell us to let go, but our minds say pleasure equates to sin. I struggled, and sometimes still struggle, to reconcile the truth that I have the freedom to express myself as a sexual creature with my husband without the guilt that wants to attach itself to those expressions. I can play, laugh, explore, and get loud when I want to, and it is good. I can say yes to pleasure and tell guilt to shut the hell up. But that takes courage.

Sometimes I see marriage and intimacy books in the Christian Living section of the bookstore that I want to take off the shelf and hide in the trash can. I don't believe in censorship, but I do believe we have a responsibility to call out harmful teaching when we see it. Sex is set apart from every other act of intimacy, and for good reason. It can cause so much harm when abused and create so much unity and life when honored. It is a holistic act of faithfulness, love, and utter delight in the image bearer you have committed yourself to for life. It is thanks to God for pleasure and connection. It is the creator of new image bearers.

But sex is not our savior or our salvation. It is where the demands of perfection need to die so that we can fully experience the wholeness of giving ourselves fully to our spouse and, through that, the holiness of being made one with God.

Sex is holy. But it is not perfect. When we can capture that truth in our minds, we get to embrace the full range of pleasure offered to us in physical intimacy, pleasure that comes from being known and knowing another, from feeling free to express ourselves without shame, and from realizing that all we knew about sex before is a joke in light of what it can be. In light of what it actually is.

We are the dearly beloved of God. Can we examine what that means? Can we meditate on our identity as the heart song of an omnipotent, all-powerful Creator? We know what it feels like to fall in love. To feel the fluttering in our stomachs, to ache for someone. Those same exciting emotions are present in God because he is responsible for their existence. God is Love—in all its forms—and he made sex to be one of the most unique and powerful ways for us to express it. For too long, we have carried unnecessary shame about the mistakes in our past and haven't known how to walk in the freedom that intimacy with God offers to us. I believe God mourns when we aren't able to experience sex with our spouse—whether it's erotic or awkward—without the specter of perfectionism haunting the corners of our minds.

I'm so tired of living in a culture that devalues intimacy for the sake of what it calls freedom. I've witnessed too many hearts crushed and too many relationships suffer because of the harm this narrative has done to us. I'm also tired of living in a culture that feels it necessary to sexualize our every experience and then damn us for daring to act on the behaviors it encourages. Most of all, I'm tired of hearing about the holy designation for sex with no one around who can be trusted enough to model it well. Those who can often don't talk about it, and the ones who can't make scandalous headlines every other week. It's no wonder Christians—least of all me—have been weighed down with so much sexual baggage.

I believe there is a way forward into wholeness and holiness, but it isn't going to be found in a culture that demands sexual freedom without spiritual connection, and it isn't going to be found among believers who shy away from it. It will be found when we dare to admit there's a lot Scripture doesn't tell us about sex. It will be found when we learn how to celebrate the ecstasy and the work required for healthy, hearty sex because, like so much in life, the complexity of a thing is what makes it beautiful. It will be found at the foot of the cross, because the cross is where the perfectionism demanded of our bodies, our abilities, and our desires died to the holiness of a God who demanded only that we love him and one another.

The cross is where love—not fear or shame or True Love Waits cards—sets us free. May this love permeate our sexual identities and our sexual experiences. May it saturate our marriages and wash away any and every thing that stands in the way of mutual pleasure and delight. May it be a continual reminder that what our culture has failed to celebrate in the bedroom—two people committed to figuring out what works, over and over again—is a beautiful, and holy, thing.

7

No Standing Ovations Here

A few years ago, I discovered from a friend that a former classmate of ours viewed me in a much different light than I viewed myself. To put it mildly. This classmate had abruptly told my friend, "Wendi was such a bitch in high school."

Not only was I confused by her statement, I was embarrassed. I had just finished telling my friend how I'd always thought our mutual acquaintance was so sweet and then discovered that she saw me that way. It was a shock to my system.

Turns out, you can try your hardest to be the right thing for every person and you'll still fail with spectacular precision.

Upon further exploration of said bitchiness, my friend told me that our classmate had sat next to me in class one semester and that I never spoke to her. I don't remember this, but then again, why would I? What seems important to us often matters little to the person seated next to us, perhaps especially in high school. At sixteen, it's close to impossible to notice what's in our peripheral vision, unless what's in our peripheral vision is someone we're attracted to, in which case we quickly shift all focus. I hadn't spoken to this girl because I hadn't realized I needed to speak to her (also, I'm a raging introvert), and because of reasons in her life my obliviousness translated as bitchiness. The truth is, I told my friend, I was stressed out about the relationship I'd been in during that time, and it would have been difficult for someone I didn't know well to pull me from the tangled spiral of what-ifs that dominated my thoughts. How could my classmate have known that? She saw what the filter of her own perspective showed her, and I had been blind to it.

I pondered on this for days. I asked my friend to share my apology with her, which he did, and she changed her tune. She learned where my head had been at sixteen, and it shifted her point of view. I could have then left it alone, but her belief that I had purposefully disregarded her did not sit well with me. Paul's words echoed in my ears: "If it is possible, as far as it depends on you, live at peace with everyone" (Rom. 12:18).

Over the years, I have often mistaken moral performance for service to others. It's true that making wise and thoughtful choices will give you a clearer conscience and a certain amount of blessing in your life. (And by "certain" I mean "I have no idea how much, but likely more than breaking the law would.") That is the nature of steering clear of harmful stuff like drugs, promiscuity, and jerks. However, it does not protect you from the opinions of others and it does not guard you against all the perils in the world, because your choices are your own. As much as you think they give you control over your life, they do not give you control over other people . . . and we live in a world where we interact with other people all day long. It is the world God designed for us. It is the conundrum of the Christian life, where our very purpose is intertwined with the purpose of our neighbor, whether we like that neighbor or not.

That we must forever walk the fine line between discipleship and being messy humans is the beauty and pain of following Jesus. Because of his service to us, we are commanded to serve others. We have valuable influence, and it is imperative that we use it well, that we walk with integrity so we do not make fools of the people who trust us. On our own, this is not a task we do well for very long.

In spite of our best efforts, we might still one day discover we were a whole bitch to someone we could not have known was harmed by our unintentional missteps. When perfect performance is the goal, service to our neighbors becomes another positive side effect of our faith, rather than the aim. Worse, at times we provide no service at all because we cannot take our eyes off ourselves. We don't notice the girl sitting next to us.

I seek security when I perform. I don't trust what it is that God has said about me without the correlation of good behavior. I deny the truth that I am already good, already holy, and in turn, I deny that truth about others. I say all the right words, but they do not pierce my heart.

When I was in middle school—a time of strife for every adolescent, and one made more so for me by difficulties in our family and my parents' bitter divorce—I took to good behavior like a duck to a pond because no matter what chaos ensued around me, I could always count on myself. I would journal my frustrations to God and cry to NSYNC albums and come out of my bedroom with all of my shit together. If no one else was going to act like good behavior was important, then I sure would.

In high school, once the chaos had settled and my parents were friends again, I latched onto good behavior because I feared the defiance of my peers would rub off on me if I didn't keep a tight grip on myself. My friends were more rebellious than I was, even if by a small margin, but I stayed in an unhealthy romantic relationship long past its expiration date because I thought of myself as the keeper of my significant other's morality. His bouts of jealousy and manipulation would stop if I could just help him see what was true and good, both about himself and about me. (This is a terrible model. Do not follow my example.) Everyone but me knew how that story would end, and by the time I got up the courage to break it off, I felt like a fool. I had policed everyone else's behavior while ignoring my own toxic choices and wasted a whole lot of time and energy in the process.

By college, I was sure I had the whole system figured out. I would leave no room for error, no possible path for me to stray. I went to my first college party adorned with a handmade Scripture bracelet that the cop who pulled me over afterward mistook for an "Over 21" band. Delighted to prove his assumptions wrong, I held out my wrist and said, "It's a Bible verse. Want to read it?" Needless to say, I walked away without a ticket.

After the end of my first adult relationship—the first one I believed would likely lead to marriage—I carried so much guilt for thinking my boyfriend's morality was still my job to secure, although in very different ways from what I had experienced in high school. I acted as if his faith and his salvation were somehow dependent on me. We enjoyed a beautiful couple of years together, but he felt restricted by me and I felt diminished by him. All the while, I quietly resented the rules of my faith. Where I had wanted life and love, I had experienced loss. The fruits I bore were of the Spirit, but they were not yet mature. There was still so much more I needed to learn.

Faith is not sustainable when it is dependent on the behavior of other people to keep it alive. This goes for boyfriends and family as much as it does for pastors and speakers. Community is an integral part of a thriving spiritual life, but when we distort community and turn people we care about into instruments of performance intended to boost our own egos, we choose rules over relationships. We choose law over love.

I got married straight out of college. And in the eleven years since that day, marriage has taught me that performance will only go so far. (It's hard to be self-righteous when you're midpoop having a discussion about the budget.) Life is about progression, not performance. Even if the steps you take forward are baby ones, you can take pride in the knowledge that you are not stagnant. It is a mistake to believe perfection is the goal when there is no such thing as arrival, at least not until we meet Jesus in the flesh. There is only growth. There is only continued transformation. There is only another lesson learned.

I'd love for us to try to release our grips a little bit. Can we learn to nourish our faith with the Water of Life, who alone secures our salvation and grants us the approval we strive to attain? Then we will see the fruit mature.

God is inviting us to taste and see that he is good. And so, my friend, are we.

CHAPTER 8

Clarity in the Chaos

If I am seated at my desk, finally settling into work that requires quiet attention to what's in front of me, it is guaranteed that my daughter will come tumbling into the room, a million questions on her lips. I know that this is not unique to me. But it never ceases to amaze me—much like it did when my mom would sixth-sense any mischievous behavior from across the house—how my child just *knows* when I finally have a solitary moment to myself.

Herein lies another problem for any perfectionist: how to do it all and do it all exceedingly well. I can't.

I have a particular way of doing things when I work. Routine doesn't matter so much as environment, and I like my space to be tidy and sweet-smelling before I can tuck into a cup of coffee and get to work. I live in a house with a husband, a kindergartner, an infant, and a Siberian husky that sheds like it's her job, so cleanliness and pleasant olfactory experiences are as much a labor as book writing or giving birth. But I chose this life. After years spent working the regular nine-to-five, I started working freelance, had a kid, and then got hired by a nonprofit that pays me to work from my couch. I have cultivated the chaos in my home after years of having it chosen for me, and sometimes I have to remind myself that this is what I signed up for.

In the seven years since I started working from home, I have come to realize that I place too high a value on keeping my exterior environment free of clutter and distractions. When neither of those things are possible, I struggle to focus on anything else. When I worked in an office, accomplishing this task was easy: I kept a coaster on my desk to prevent coffee stains and all my folders organized in neat rows in my drawer. But being a working mother means not only working to make a living but also working amid noise and inconvenience. Interruptions are more than just guaranteed; they're constant.

I know that when my children are older I will miss the sweet and brutal chaos of raising them. It certainly takes a sense of humor to do the job and, recently, I chose to step away from the scrolling time-suck that is social media for a bit so I could actually feel confident about my ability to be a mom and wife. It was not easy. I love Instagram almost as much as I love coffee. (And if you've ever seen my Instagram page, you know my love for coffee borders on obsession.) I had been posting daily for five years and it wasn't sustainable anymore. I don't need to repeat what we all know about social media these days. Anyone who uses it is aware of how contradictory it can make us feel, both about the people we love and about ourselves. I fell in love with so many wonderful things because of social media, but I kind of fell out of love with my own life.

Moms, we're so hard on ourselves. We manage to keep our children alive and (mostly) safe each day and sometimes we even have good sex with our husbands at night, but all we can think about is whether or not the house will ever be exactly what we pictured (or what we saw in a picture) or if we bought enough organic vegetables or if the amount of commercials baby girl saw this morning means she will become a spoiled materialistic brat by the age of six. One of my new mom friends told me just yesterday that we need to stop giving each other advice all the time and just tell the moms in our lives that they're doing a good job. Forgetting for a moment that my friend seems to have a better handle on motherhood after eighteen months than I do after six years, I tend to agree with her.

Moms, you're doing a good job.

You applied for this position and when God said, "You're hired!" he meant it. Besides the obvious, I don't know how the whole process works because I am not the Creator of the universe, but if you are a mother—whether you mother biological babies or foster kiddos or beloved nieces and nephews or groups of teenagers who look up to you when they have no one else—it's because you have been entrusted with the privilege. I am convinced that there is no such thing as an inherently bad mother. Just as every single child is born flawed but without sin, mothers are born into the parenting game with a clean slate, regardless of past mistakes or current circumstances. Even if you've believed the worst about yourself for a while, there is still hope, my friend. There are still more good moments to be had, the next right choice to be made. That is the beauty of God's grace; we don't have to wait to begin anew in the morning. We can start over this very second and keep starting over until the moment we take our last breath. Sometimes that truth is the only thing that gets me through the day.

Last night, during Bible study with my husband, one of the study questions asked us to identify a hope that we have full confidence entrusting to God. I answered my work. I expected something similar from Pierce, perhaps something like his work or friendships, but he surprised me by saying, "The way you care for Lucy and Theo. I never doubt when I walk out that door each morning that they'll have whatever they need from you."

Okay, my husband has always been a sweetheart, but you could have knocked me over with a feather if I hadn't already been seated.

Since I'm a person who relies heavily on words of affirmation, this was a surprising and sweet balm to the wounds I inflict on myself constantly, to the second-guessing that plays its bitter refrain over the soundtrack of my days far more often than it should.

Do you need to hear that truth as well? Well, here it is: You have everything you need to be exactly the mother your child requires. You also have everything you need to be the wife or friend or sister your loved ones are seeking. You have everything you need to live out who you already are.

The scrutiny on women is at a fever pitch, the reasons of which are complicated and almost certainly include the aforementioned complexities of social media. If we have them, we are expected to entertain our children all day while also getting our work done and still, somehow, maintain our figures, homes, marriages, friendships, and the million other responsibilities that fall at our feet. We're also supposed to do this primarily on our own and in a way that manages to please every person we meet, regardless of that person's background or experience. You'd be hard-pressed to find people who'd demand that verbatim, but the impression remains even if it's not explicitly stated.

We need our villages. We were made for community, and motherhood is no exception. Who among us has gone a single week of parenthood or marriage without reaching for the wisdom and comfort of a trusted loved one? Where did the ridiculous lie first rear its ugly head, telling us that independence in all things is the way to go?

Being a parent is really, really hard, and doing it alone is even harder. Gay or straight, single or married, there is not a single person in this world who doesn't long for companionship in some regard. It's the way we were designed, and it's a good thing. If you have it, friend, use it. Call on your spouse or partner. Call on your people. They were made for you just as surely as you were made for them. God is a giver of good gifts, and our people are near the very top of that list.

In the end, I believe being a mother is good and holy work. I will not deny that. I also don't believe it is a woman's highest or even her holiest work. There are so many for whom motherhood didn't pan out exactly as they'd hoped and, yet, those of us in the church still find ourselves thinking that the primary option for a full and abundant life is a full and abundant uterus. God's command for us to wholly love him and others as ourselves can be fulfilled in innumerable ways, and when we as women are convinced that becoming moms—or attempting to become perfect moms—is the only route to spiritual wholeness, we are robbed of our ability to even love ourselves.

This is no small feat to overcome, I know. Every message we receive from birth seems to revolve around a woman's worth being found in her physical body: what she can do with it, what she should or shouldn't do with it, how beautiful/coiffed/toned/curvy/skinny it is. The world makes little room for imperfection. But God uses our imperfections to create beautiful, extraordinary things.

If I were to tally them up, I could name a hundred ways I fall short of the mark every day. More often than not, though, my perceived failures are less about things I've done wrong and more about how much time I've wasted thinking I could be better.

But Jesus didn't demand that we be better in order to be good. He just said, "Follow me." Even if you're stumbling after him, falling down over bumps in the road, you're in his wake.

The work that waits for me at home each day is, as they say, sanctifying. That is the essence of work, whether it's in a smelly office or a sleek boardroom. The roles we've chosen to live, which for me include marriage and motherhood but might look very different for you, are vital. To rise and give ourselves to the demands of the day, to keep at it no matter how many times we are distracted or interrupted or afraid, is participation in the glory of the kingdom. Finishing a page of this book—when all I really want to do is avoid the challenge of arranging twenty-six letters into combinations people find worthwhile—is glorious. Doing it in an office that smells a little like our dog crate, because all my candles have been burnt to charred remains and I can't pretend otherwise, is even more so. If I could make every moment of my life smell like apple cinnamon and feel as satisfying as the closing of a chapter I've been writing for weeks, I would be more than tempted to do so.

The clarity comes in the chaos. The glory arrives alongside the interruptions. The sanctification shows up with the surrender.

No matter how much you think you're failing, I say, keep doing the work. There is no one who can do yours the way you will.

CHAPTER 9
Welcome Home

I go to a big church. The biggest in Atlanta, in fact. Most people call it a "mega" church, but for most of our membership years, it has felt more like home to me than any other church—big or small—I've ever attended.

Northpoint Ministries launched back in 1995 when Andy Stanley broke from his father's church and, with the support of a handful of committed members, began to hold Sunday services in rented facilities. Eventually, they saved enough to build their first official home, and Northpoint Community Church opened its doors in the fall of 1998. In 2001, the church expanded to a new campus in Buckhead, just north of Atlanta, and has since grown to include seven metro Atlanta campuses and almost a hundred more partner churches across the world. In 2010, a college buddy of mine invited me to attend the Easter service at Northpoint to hear Andy preach. Months later, after my husband and I grew tired of watching pastors teach questionable sermons on television every Sunday, we decided to attend a service at Buckhead Church. By summer's end, we had become members of a small group, and by the next spring I was volunteering with the high school ministry. We became official members that same year and threw ourselves—quite literally body and soul—into this local, and very large, congregation.

In early 2011, Andy preached a series called "Big Church." For weeks, he walked us through the New Testament book of Acts, through stories about the women and men of the first century who sacrificed dearly in order to ensure the Good News reached the world. I took feverish notes. I had never heard anyone humanize members of the early church in quite this way, using humor and historical context to pump blood through their veins. For the first time in my life, the disciples John and Peter were real people. For the first time, I heard the story of Priscilla and listened as women were called disciples, too, their inclusion in the church and individual conversions on equal footing with that of the men. Their devotion to Jesus and to the mission of the Gospel meant I could sit in that sanctuary and hear their names, their sacrifices, their extraordinary courage. Because of what the Lord had done through those early *ekklesias*, the body of Christ had grown into a worldwide assembly of believers. It had, indeed, become a Big Church, and we were a crucial part of it on both a global and local scale.

I had never thought too much about the size of a congregation carrying any particular meaning, but suddenly my membership in a "mega" church made me the receiver of comments that ranged in intensity from "I could never go to a church that big" and "Don't you want your pastor to know who you are?" to "Those places only want your money" and "That guy is a heretic." It seemed, much to my surprise, that lots of people equated more members in a church with less community, skewed theology, and wasted resources.

Perhaps like you, I have attended church in a variety of Christian traditions over the course of my life: nondenominational, Catholic, Episcopalian, Lutheran, Reformed Presbyterian, Baptist, Methodist, Church of God, and more. I grew up in a midsize nondenominational church with a charismatic influence, and later became a member of the large Baptist congregation in my hometown. In college, I sometimes attended Catholic services with my boyfriend on the weekend and went to Tuesday services on campus at the Baptist Student Union. I took issue with the Catholic view on baptism but, in general, never gave the difference in these traditions much thought.

As an adult, I have grown to love the way that believers—across the world and across my city—seek to connect with their heavenly Father. The liturgies of mainline churches seem to reflect something ancient in the way a whole assembly of voices raised in repetition call out the mystery and majesty of God. Baptist hymns touch the deep part of my soul where the childhood version of myself lives, where melody and Southern accents move together like molasses, sweet and heavy. Pentecostals have taught me that the Holy Spirit is still alive and well, moving in ways that continue to surprise and upend what I believe about how God works. In every tradition, we love the Lord. In every congregation, there is a place to know something new about him. This is the nature of community, the heartbeat of gathering together as one body.

And, y'all, I love my Big Church. We attend a smaller campus on the east side of the city now, housed in a renovated church building we share with two other congregations. Every Sunday, we walk those crowded concrete halls with our children, wave to friendly faces, and drop them off in their classrooms where they, too, will partake in worship, be it songs from a stage or the comforting hum of a caretaker as she rocks my son to sleep. We head to the front of the sanctuary (because I love a good front-row seat) where we worship to gospel classics, jazzed-up versions of contemporary hits, and soulful hymns performed with vocal runs like you wouldn't believe. We are spoiled by the musical talent of believers in this city, and I sob into my shirt sleeve on the regular.

The corporate nature of the church is its most precious gift. We continue to come together because the message of Jesus bewilders and compels us, his sacrifice for his children so unbelievable, and so good, that we can't help but return to it. On the flip side, the church as a whole can be, and has been, hurtful to us because it is made up of people. Of sinners. We are good, but we are not God, and so we fail. We gossip. We exclude. We reject. We also forgive, choose mercy, and see God put lives and stories back together that we once believed irreparable. The healing nature of the body is experienced only after wounds have been inflicted, and this is the dichotomy we wrestle with daily. We cannot know how much injury has been avoided because we can never know what hasn't been—what terrible injustice didn't happen because the church was there—but the not knowing doesn't negate the truth. The church has accomplished immeasurable good in the world and, one day, when this life is over, we will see just how much. And we will marvel.

I have so much hope for us, for the "us" God says we are. We are mighty in his name and we are lambs in need of our shepherd. We are disciples and pastors and leaders, and we are students of the Word made flesh. We are cocreators with Christ, and we are children of God.

Despite all the problems—and I think I've been honest about some of the problems I've had in churches and in church contexts—I believe we return to our churches again and again because we know, be it by conscious or unconscious thought, that they are places of hope. I see this during baptisms when members share their stories, stories that often include some stepping away from either their local church or the corporate church for a season. The wounds needed to heal, and God provides that healing when a person steps back into a faith community—new or old—and says, "You hurt me, but I belong here."

In these tender, vulnerable spaces, I've seen people hold out their hands and say, "Yes, you do belong here. Welcome." I've watched as believers who were terrified of entering a sanctuary again find safe haven.

Here in Atlanta, the initial anonymity of my Big Church can be helpful for those who want to test the waters, who aren't sure if all will indeed be well once people know their stories. The anonymity doesn't last long for those who choose to hope. Because of God's faithfulness through the thousands of other believers who have invested into their local faith communities, someone who once vowed never to go back can find a place to truly, wholly belong. It is the gift of an imperfect body made holy. It is the story we know well, and long to know better, the story of a Redeemer about his business of redeeming.

My memories of church while growing up are good ones, but I know this isn't the case for others in my family or perhaps even for you. I was so young when we broke from our home church, and while I know what happened to cause the break, I was never exposed to those hurts directly. My memories are of my dad playing drums on stage and singing "Mary, Did You Know?" during the holidays, of my mom interpreting our pastor's sermons in a dark blue suit, her long blond hair curled into large ringlets. I remember being awed by the fact that my mother, who couldn't carry a tune in a bucket, could interpret worship music so beautifully it brought tears to every eye in the congregation. I remember the large Black family who sat in front of us and whose extended family members took up three whole rows. I remember their humor and faith, their incredible vocal range, and the rhythm with which they worshiped. I remember longing for their kind of joy.

When I got older, I found out how some members of our church had mistreated my mother because of her beauty and unsettled faith. She'd had a tumultuous childhood and asked a lot of questions about God, questions that were not always well-received. She also had the audacity to love her body in a place where above-the-knee skirts earned one the side eye, and eventually a church that had brought us so much good became a place of deep unrest for our family. I visited it for the last time on Easter Sunday during my sophomore year of high school, and even on that day, years after we had moved our membership, there was division in our family about the legacy our former church home had left for us.

These memories were on my mind when I moved my membership from the Baptist church in my hometown to Buckhead. After my parents left the church I'd grown up attending, nothing ever seemed to fit. In my young adult years, I was a devout believer without a place to believe in. I read my Bible at home, scribbled prayers in my journal, and called it church. I talked theology and Jesus with my best guy friend. I devoured faith memoirs and books about Christ and finished them with a fiery dissatisfaction about the state of my own faith. The presence of the Holy Spirit was palpable, her voice inaudible but constant, a reminder that more was available to me if I wanted it. So I kept reading. I kept praying. I kept writing. Still, the longing persisted.

In that tender spring season when we first heard Andy preach, the longing finally settled. As the world around us woke up from her winter slumber and bloomed with new life, I celebrated a homecoming. Here, in this Big Church, we were embraced as though we had always belonged, and the physical stature of the church itself seemed to shrink alongside our continued presence in it. We began to recognize more and more people each Sunday and, as time passed, we transitioned from churchgoers to church members, unconscious of exactly when the internal shift had occurred but very much conscious that it had.

The way our culture treats church right now—as though it should belong on some sort of faith community dating app where we swipe left or right depending on our myriad of preferences—is harmful to our spiritual health. I do not advocate for our continued membership in a church where we are not valued, heard, or included. I do not advocate for spiritual abuse. I advocate for a body that tends to itself with the recognition that it isn't perfect, that not every church experience will meet expectations, and that no matter where we are, the church will always fail to meet our standards exactly as we propose them, just as we will always fail to follow the rules as God proposed them. This is where we get to practice supernatural grace for our sisters and brothers who work in ministry, who have the great task of shepherding the unique and diverse needs of their congregations.

I don't have much experience in church operations, what goes on from day to day. Pierce and I have volunteered for a number of roles and ministries in our Big Church over the last decade, and have been a part of the behind-the-scenes action, but we are still far removed from the inner workings of the church as an organization. I imagine it can be tedious, stressful, and mundane. What looks effortless in a classroom or on a stage is the result of many hours of manpower. The message we hear preached comes after countless days of research and prayer and writing and rewriting, and that on top of years of experience and education. The amount of resources and support available to children, teenagers, college students, and adults—all from vastly different homes, backgrounds, and lives—is in direct correlation to the generosity of the church members. How any church gets from one day to the next, how my beloved Big Church gets from one day to the next, is really nothing short of a miracle.

Every church is a miracle. The fact that we found one we can call our home is a miracle. Perhaps your miracle is that you still love Jesus even though your church failed you. I am confident that there is still room for you here, in a church, where traditions may divide but Christ unites. This is where we become holy, together, and where we continue to hope.

Hope that God is still working all things together for the good of those who love him. Hope that our efforts to show up to a faith community—in a big concrete building or in a friend's home—are not in vain. Hope that we are not simply checking the box and calling ourselves even with God, but believing that God is there with and among us—Emmanuel—for we are not just the result of his great love.

We are God's great love.

10
Redefining Good

One of the first things Pierce and I did as a married couple after joining our Big Church was jump headfirst into a small group (also known as a Bible study, or community group). At the time, we were one of a small handful of couples our age who were married, and we were somewhat desperate to make friends with other married couples in Atlanta.

Our first small group was made of five couples. We were all from different parts of the country and we brought a wide range of faith perspectives to the group, but we had in common a few very important things: none of us were parents yet and we all loved Jesus. We clicked in a way we had been warned might not happen, and I sometimes think it's because of this first valuable small-group experience that Pierce and I became more invested in our church. It's natural to come to a small group and find out that it's not the best fit, which is why our model suggests a six-week warm-up period for people to work through any issues that might arise or step away if they need to, along with a two-year max for every group. People naturally tend to merge into different phases of life around that time, which we found to be true, but not before we first found lifelong friends.

Ours is a big world. We are surrounded by information and noise that we can tap into at any moment, almost anywhere. For the most part, this is a benefit. It builds our capacity for entrepreneurship and knowledge, for technological advancement and accessibility. The internet has, in many ways, put people on equal footing. If you have a smart device and some decent wifi, you can create, build, and access more than generations before us even thought to dream about, much less do.

And yet so much of life is lived in the small moments, the moments between people connected in person. Nothing can ever fully replace the sound of a loved one's voice or the feel of their touch. No one can like you or care about your success the way a friend invested in the unseen moments can. We know this to be true no matter how much we enjoy our phones. What momentary comfort is felt from scrolling and clicking will, at some point, leave us with the same hollow fullness we get from gorging on a pint of ice cream. Sure, it's delicious, but we are still hungry for more.

In our two years together as a small group, we dealt with the pressure of first jobs and grad school, questions of parenthood and adoption, successes and failures and moves and more. The guys were sharp and ambitious, quirky and quick-witted. The women were creative and bright, full of big ideas and big hearts. I loved them all. Our small group became our sounding board, and every Sunday we squeezed into whichever apartment was home base that night and devoured cheese plates and fruit trays with a generous side of conversation, debate, and prayer. Every week I went home after those meetings surprised by the depth of my affection for those people— who had in just a few short months become beloved friends—and the transformation of my heart into a more empathetic, less dogmatic, one. Our small group thawed a hardness in me I hadn't even been aware of until it started to disappear.

It's a strange experience to come up against one's own misconceptions. How unnerving it can be to discover that all you once believed to be black and white is really much more complex than you knew. For some, this realization feels like freedom, but there have been times when it felt to me like another burden to carry. I don't know what it's like to lose my faith or to meet Jesus for the first time as an adult, but I do know that when you sit down face-to-face with people who think differently from you, the answers you've carried in your heart with such confidence begin to transform into more questions. This can grieve us, or it can move us closer toward God and each other.

Sometimes, it does both.

• ˙ **•••**
•

In the Gospel accounts of Matthew, Mark, Luke, and John, we see close friends and followers of Jesus grapple with the transformation of their faith. For thousands of years, it had been marked by an omniscient and unknowable God who, with the exception of a unique few, remained distant. He was everywhere and nowhere, all-powerful and seemingly difficult to please.

Then came Jesus, who transformed everything people thought they understood about what God wanted from his children.

In his Sermon on the Mount, Jesus offered people a perspective on obedience to God that allowed for frailties, mistakes, and forgiveness in ways that must have been uncomfortable for the first people who heard him. At first glance, it can seem as though Jesus was adding more to their plates, particularly when he said, "For I tell you that unless your righteousness surpasses that of the Pharisees and the teachers of the law, you will certainly not enter the kingdom of heaven" (Matt. 5:20). Oof. I can imagine hearing this and thinking, "You want me to be more righteous than the most righteous people we know? Hard pass." It's what I think now when someone demands more from me.

"I'm tired," I want to say. "I can't keep up with your expectations no matter how hard I try." And that's the point. Jesus was not telling his followers to do more and be better. He was telling them to be his.

The law didn't cease to reflect the nature of God when Jesus came along. It just ceased to be the primary way in which we obey and live in relationship with God. I know people who get stuck on this passage from the Gospel of John, in which Jesus states, "If you love me, keep my commands" (14:15). A few verses later, Jesus repeats himself: "Anyone who loves me will obey my teaching" (14:23). We minimize these verses and remove their heart when we mistake them for demands that we become better rule followers. In this way, they become lifeless and result in lifeless faith.

Just prior to making these statements, Philip had asked Jesus to show him and the other disciples what God was like, and Jesus replied, in what I imagine was a tender and somewhat exasperated tone, "Don't you know me, Philip, even after I have been among you such a long time?" (John 14:9). There is so much human intimacy in this moment. Jesus is looking at a friend, just as we would, and asking if his friend has been paying attention. "Believe me when I say that I am in the Father and the Father is in me. . . . Very truly I tell you, whoever believes in me will do the works I have been doing, and they will do even greater things than these, because I am going to the Father" (John 14:11–12).

Can't we see? This is not another list of demands, but a declaration of hope. Jesus offered us the gift of his righteousness in exchange for our belief in him. He told us obedience comes not from being rule-obsessed, but from something more, something much more personal. It comes from love. Love makes a way for us to know Jesus and to know each other, and Jesus is the way we live out the fullness of this good, good life. There is no rule or law that can do what he has done.

We have the Holy Spirit, the One who "teaches you all things and will remind you of everything I have said to you" (John 14:26). We need these reminders to keep our legalism in check, to shove aside our preconceived notions about each other, and to reveal the sorry state of our self-righteous hearts so that love can remove the obstacles keeping us, just like Philip, from recognizing God when we see him.

Living small, with love at the epicenter of my faith, opens my eyes to the presence of God inside my fellow believers. Some people, myself included, fear that love will not answer the questions we so long to answer. We come with timid hearts, eager to know God more but with conditions about what—or who—he might introduce us to. We want to love Jesus and are disconcerted to discover that loving him is a package deal. We cannot know him without also knowing the people he created.

In the Gospels, we find that love is the answer. This is not trite nonsense. It is a truth so magnificent that we struggle to come to terms with it because we are simply not God. To us, love is fluff and feelings. Love is as changeable as the wind and as unreliable too. It is shifting sand, and we would be wise not to build our houses on it. Apart from Jesus, love is just an emotion. But John, the last living disciple, wrote in the New Testament letter attributed to him that God's very identity is love (1 John 4:8), and if we try to define it by our own inability to live it well, we will forever disregard it as the shallow stuff of poorly written romance novels.

"This is love," John wrote. "Not that we loved God, but that he loved us . . ." (1 John 4:10). He loved us. I am learning, again and again, that I, too, want to love what God loves. I, too, want this four-letter word to be my very identity.

For a long time, I was quite uncomfortable with the shift in my faith. You'd think my waning desire to correct other people would calm my anxious spirit, but it did the opposite. I was disconcerted by this change because it wasn't simply a change in my behavior; it was a change in me as a person. I felt afraid, at times, that if I didn't speak up about someone's perceived sins, then I would be held accountable for them, and this was the crux of the issue. This was the fulcrum that needed to turn so I could stop seeing my friends and family through critical eyes and start seeing them through compassionate ones. God had not given me the job of moral management, as I had believed for so long, but the privilege of service. This was a foreign concept. Service was a thing to do, an obligatory act of obedience, not a way of life. As I had learned about a myriad of other actions connected to my spiritual health, service was altogether different from what I had long believed it to be, and the Lord was going to help me work out my salvation with fear and trembling no matter what.

We continued to invest in our local church. We led more adult groups and then moved on to the high school ministry. My initial attempt to lead a high school small group, which is an enormous commitment involving a four-year investment in students from freshman to senior year, had been cut short. I had made it almost a year and then chose to stop because I was in grad school and working full-time while Pierce and I were searching for a house. All of this was happening while my OCD was in high gear, and it was simply too much to try to tackle at once. I was in overdrive and had nothing left to give my students.

A few years later, after we'd been in our house for a while and our daughter, Lucy, was a bit older, I jumped in once more. Pierce had been leading a group of middle school students for three years and they were moving onto ninth grade, so we became high school leaders at the same time.

Those four years as a high school small-group leader didn't reveal much about God I didn't already believe, but they revealed a lot about the way God is moving on behalf of future generations. I witnessed the girls in my group confess closely guarded secrets and hold each other up with grace and not a single batted eye. I listened as they expressed righteous anger about injustice and inequality alongside diatribes about boys and catty classmates. I cried and vented frustration over their long, unexplained absences from group, but my heart swelled over their returns just like any mother's would. I learned that we can expect young adults to carve out more space for God than any generation before them because they see him in places—and people—others do not. As a student leader, I had to exercise my trust muscle and remember my only job was to show up and keep showing up, no matter how tired or discouraged I was.

In Matthew, Jesus tells his followers, "Let your light shine before others, that they may see your good deeds and glorify your Father in heaven" (5:16). A couple of years into student leadership, I thought perhaps my good deeds needed a makeover. I didn't suddenly believe my values were out of alignment with God's, but I did start to envision a new kind of goodness for myself, the kind where the blessed were not moral missionaries intent on perfect performance but people who were merciful peacemakers, humble to the point of Christ, who made himself nothing on earth even when he had every right to reign.

So my coleader and I began to embrace the gift of being present, the privilege of stewardship over our students' tender hearts whether we were all laughing together at the beach or sitting in a mostly empty meeting room. They grew into young women who stun me day after day, leaders in their own spaces and disciples of a bigger, more beautiful God than the One I experienced at their age.

As a child, I used to tell my parents I wanted to go to heaven at the age of twelve because I simply couldn't wait any longer to be in the presence of the Lord. I knew this world was full of lovely things, thanks to the devotion and tender care of my mom and dad, but still my desire for more could not be fulfilled. Twelve years on earth was my limit, and then I wanted to go home where I would never fail to live up to my own expectations ever again. Even as a child, I knew this world would not satisfy me no matter how many wonderful gifts it contained. And I have been lucky, for it has contained many. But God was not content to bring me home in my ignorance. He has required that I learn the difference between my own false expectations of perfection and the gift of his holiness time and time again, and I suspect I will continue learning this lesson until he decides I've had enough.

We must leave ourselves open to God's upending. It can feel a bit like an itchy wool sweater, which protects and warms us but remains uncomfortable no matter how we twist and fidget. But discomfort is not the same as destruction.

Relationships with other believers, particularly when our faith is in transition, can secure the swaying edifice upon which we have stood for however long we've loved the Lord. Still, the very people who cause us to see God as bigger, mightier, and more inclusive can also be the catalyst for our new uncertainties. This is typical of people like me who used to equate the straight and narrow path with a straight and narrow God, an easily labeled and easily frustrated cosmic judge. We needn't fear these new, unexplored paths as though they will divert us from the truth. God cannot be made smaller by broader views, for as many types of Jesus followers there are who walk this earth, there are an equal number of angles from which to see him. He does not stop being God because we learn to look at him with different eyes. From the vantage point of believers like me who once held our own singular views in the highest regard, when I open myself to the discomfort of a new perspective, Jesus actually becomes more fully what Scripture tells us he is, what I've always hoped he would be: Way, Truth, and Life.

The Way to a holiness without striving because Christ alone is our righteousness. The Truth about who we are regardless of how well we check the boxes and follow the rules dictated by the faith we grew up in. The Life abundant, glory be, as the children of a God who would leave the ninety-nine to chase after the one.

Part Three

Undoing Perfect

CHAPTER 11

God for Sale

I cringed as the creative director told me the script wasn't strong enough.

"You've got to really sell it," he told me, another coffee in his hand, his fifth since that morning. "People won't give unless they feel like they're missing something. They have to believe that if they don't call that number, some opportunity or answered prayer will fly right out the window."

I rolled my eyes. This was not what I'd had in mind when I took a job writing for a faith-based media company. Call me naive, but I had thought there would be a bit more gospel and a little less prosperity in our work. Silly me.

"But that's not true," I countered, defensive of my script as well as the audience who'd be hearing it from their recliners. "That's not how God works."

"It's how we work," he told me, matter-of-fact. "You have to sell God if you want people to buy him."

Gross.

I went to work every day and racked my brain for how I could rebel against the capitalistic language my boss wanted me to use in our scripts. If he suggested I tell the audience to send in a love gift (money) to claim God's favor and defeat the lie of "less than" (I can't even type that without gagging), I would soften it with a phrase like "Jesus will never withhold anything from you he has already promised!" My goal was vague, religious rhetoric that viewers could connect to, whatever their circumstance. I knew there weren't any people in the audience dissecting my words, but I did all I could to manipulate the script toward a living, breathing Jesus and away from a genie in the sky who could be bought with the words of a televangelist asking for money in his Tom Ford suit. Sometimes the creative director balked, and I got yelled at. Sometimes they loved it and I celebrated my victory with an inward monologue about how their whole farce would go up in smoke one day. I wondered if this was how Jesus felt about the merchants in the temple. As I didn't have a table to flip, I flipped scripts instead.

Part of what makes Christianity so accessible and attractive is grace. We all need it and we all want it and it's so, so hard to give, especially when we believe we have the moral upper hand. I thought my coworkers were cool people, in general, but the way the company operated smacked hard of self-importance and looked almost nothing like the Jesus we claimed to follow. I spoke up often and annoyed my boss to no end. It was a mutual annoyance. He was there to do a job; I was there to boost my portfolio and help people. In the end, I did neither, and less than two years after I was hired, I was out of a job.

I didn't personally dislike my boss; I just didn't respect his ethics. He and others above him seemed to view God as a pawn in their own professional game, and while I never saw it pan out for them the way they wanted, there are others for whom this kind of faith-based manipulation has brought undeniable wealth, fame, and success.

My heart grieves as I watch people use Jesus as a tool to pander to those of us who want to serve him, preying on our weaknesses to do so. My grief grows as I question how we are blind to what's happening. I'm glad my job writing scripts only lasted eighteen months, but I have not forgotten my role in those ministries of manipulation. How many people called that number on the screen and gave what they had, only to receive empty promises as a result? Whose faith faltered because they sought help the only way they knew how and came away with a broken heart? God, forgive me for my participation, however unwilling, in such mockery.

This is a battle that rages on. We buy a caricature of God hoping for the real thing, and at times it can be hard to spot the lies when they're packaged in such beautiful detail. I love to learn, and I read books, watch movies, and scroll blogs with a critical eye, eager to spot the hook upon which we've been asked to hang our faith and test it for its strength. This is a wise course to take, to pray for wisdom and apply it thoughtfully to our consumption of media and messages. It is also necessary if we want to avoid building our faith on sand.

At night, when my brain tends to whirl instead of rest, I sometimes think about people I tried to save with rules about God. Because I erred on the side of caution and played it safe, I stayed out of trouble. I do not regret those choices and am grateful I walked out of my adolescence and into adulthood with few regrets, but I know I hurt people in the process. In my attempts to help, I harmed because I made it my mission to correct instead of love. I thought they were one and the same, but that's not the case in every circumstance. Part of loving people well means recognizing we are not their saviors and that there will be seasons when the best way for us to be salt and light is by asking the question that has donned evangelical wrists since the early nineties: "What would Jesus do?"

My work for that faith-based media company revealed that I was complicit in manipulation. I sold God by hawking good behavior. Who bought my wares and ended up missing out on Jesus altogether? These are questions that should concern anyone who is intent on obedience to Christ. If the gospel includes a message that promotes adherence to a particular church tradition over a confession of Jesus as king, then it needs to be reviewed. If the gospel touts a message about the exclusivity of the faith—who is welcome, who is not—over the inclusivity of us as one body, one bride under the sovereignty of Jesus, in whom there is "neither Jew nor Gentile, neither slave nor free, nor is there male and female, for you are all one in Christ Jesus" (Gal. 3:28), then it needs to be tossed out. Our theology matters. Our study of Scripture and continued education about the history of the church is necessary and adds to the fullness of our faith. But only Jesus justifies and declares the ungodly righteous.

Only Jesus makes us holy.

We are the handiwork of God, and everything created by God is good. Even when we're searching elsewhere for something or someone to satisfy our needs, our searching is evidence of God's thumbprint on us. Our answers might not align with his, but our persistent longing for depth, fullness, and the kind of joy that lasts reflects his heart. It seems to me that the problem isn't that we don't want the things God wants; the problem is that we have forgotten we are those things.

Before I left my job, I sat through a number of long meetings in which the head of the company railed against the evils of liberalism. He wasn't off-base with some of his concerns, but I watched him work himself into a frenzy over what he could not control. It was obvious that he wrestled with how to steward his faith and live out the call of discipleship. In his fits of anxiety, I saw myself, and I felt compassion for both his nerves and his restless spirit, which every person on his staff had to endure. He was at once earnest in his desire to do good and critical of anyone who did not fall in line with his particular brand of faith, and this was a challenge I empathized with in spite of my disdain for how he lived it out at work. It was a toxic environment and I was glad to be rid of it. It also reminded me to consider my own pursuit of goodness with mindfulness toward the people who could be tricked into the belief that they must earn their salvation.

God doesn't need us to market him like we're brand ambassadors. Jesus is the Author and Perfector of our faith, the One who writes our stories and sanctifies us, and none of this is possible without him. We are to be light for the world to bear witness to a God who gave himself for our transgressions, and we need that God if we are to be any good at it.

How glorious it is to be a child of God! Our roles here are a privilege. Our lives are a gift from the Lord because he longs for us to know his extravagant, outrageous, unconditional love. How different might our culture and our churches be if we stopped acting as if faith is a box to check and considered this privilege in the workplace, on stage, online, and in the home? How might we guard ourselves against those who try to convince us otherwise for the sake of their own pocketbooks? How much freer would we be without the fear that keeps us from perfect love?

God is not in need of salespeople. God will not cease to be God if we aren't promoting him. But people all across the world might never know the wild and unfathomable love of Jesus if we—his beloved children—allow ourselves to be bought by the highest bidder and forget who we are.

CHAPTER 12

Waking Up to Lies

Like many other white, well-intentioned, middle-class Christians, I once applied—and was accepted—to go on a service trip to Kenya. I had just finished reading a book about selling all my worldly possessions to go and make disciples and realized I was not accurately playing my part. It has taken some time, but over the years I have discovered I'm easy to manipulate if you show me arguments that my work is essential to the salvation of every person on earth.

Thankfully, the organization responsible for our Kenya trip works to provide for needs from indigenous church leadership on the ground in countries where they partner together. I'm grateful for that now. Back then, I would have had no problem playing white savior because I thought it was my job. (Decolonizing my worldview is a long, necessary road I've just begun to walk.)

The day I was accepted onto the team, I was in my third week of a new, stressful job and hadn't thought I would garner a spot. So on top of wrangling with my boss about taking ten days off work after less than six months of employment, I also had the insurmountable task of raising over four thousand dollars to fund my trip. Somehow, over the course of six months and with the help of hundreds of generous people, I managed to cover the cost.

If you've ever traveled to Africa, you know about the vaccinations. Included on the list of numerous shots required of each trip member was a malaria medication. At the health department, I was given three options: I could take the daily pill, the weekly pill, or the antibiotic. I chose the weekly pill, which I was required to begin at least one month prior to the trip and continue for two weeks after.

On the day of our departure, I felt moody. For weeks, I had lived beneath a little black rain cloud, and I couldn't sort out why. I was so excited about this trip and the work we'd be doing and had spent months prepping and praying. The shift in my emotional state was entirely unwelcome. I couldn't shake it no matter how many funny movies I watched on the plane or how much I prayed, and by the time we arrived in Nairobi, a full twenty-four hours after we left Atlanta, I was already longing for home.

I don't like to overspiritualize mental illness. It is complex and involves a variety of environmental, behavioral, physical, emotional, and spiritual variables. My OCD is hard-wired into my brain, but the brain is not unchangeable. Since the enemy knows our physical weaknesses, he prowls like a lion on the hunt searching for a way to attack us when we are vulnerable. My mental health is a biological thing, but the way it manifests and how much it impacts my life is very much a spiritual one.

The combination of the malaria medication, isolation from my husband, lack of sleep, and my OCD triggered what was essentially a ten-day-long panic attack. I couldn't sleep at night for fear that I would hurt my roommate. I would lie on my twin bed, feet away from where she slept, and press my fingers into the mattress or the wall to ground me and prove that I was still in bed and not smothering my roommate with a pillow. I also tucked the mosquito netting under the bed so that, in the morning, I could see whether or not it had been disturbed. (Kind of like how our middle school teachers used to tape

the outside of our hotel room doors when we'd go on overnight trips.)
After two nights of tossing and turning until the early hours of dawn,
I managed to snag an extra bed in the leader's room where there were
three other women sleeping. Being with a larger group gave me some
comfort at night, and they graciously agreed, night after night, to let
me sleep there. They didn't prod me with questions, but I could tell
they were confused about my behavior, so I tried to phrase my reasons
in the least dramatic way possible. My poor roommate told me later
that she just assumed I hated her.

Nope, I thought. *I was just scared I'd murder you in my sleep.*

Our trip was lovely, but the beauty of it was constantly marred by
the fog in which I walked. I could hear what people said to me, and I
could see the landscapes that surrounded us, but I couldn't download
them to my brain. I was out of storage space, space that was being
occupied by a rapidly multiplying colony of intrusive thoughts I could
neither wish away nor ignore.

Upon waking each morning, I would sigh in relief that I had made
it through the night, that I had slept a least a few hours and that
everyone on my team was still alive. But the relief was short-lived
and usually only lasted until lunch. After that, I would start worrying
about how to ask our team leader if I could spend yet another night in
her room because trying again to sleep in my own bed was completely
out of the question. By the time we'd be on the bus driving back to our
hotel, my heart would be pounding so hard I would look down and be
able to see the palpitations beneath my left breast.

Dinner was the worst because after dinner followed a team
meeting and bedtime. I love food—new food, weird food, all food—
and I barely ate more than one full meal a day, so focused I was on
the thoughts I couldn't control. I lost eight pounds in just over a week

and knew that every moment spent obsessing was another moment of this once-in-a-lifetime trip I was missing. I just couldn't make myself care. All I cared about was surviving the trip and making it home to my husband so I could forget any of it had ever happened.

When you're drowning, you either want to get out alive or die a quick death. The threat, and the outcome of the threat, is all that matters. Making sense of what's happening is only the blessing of survival.

Well, I survived. And I learned that sometimes you don't want to make sense of what's happening, because the shock of what you've endured—the fear you believed would kill you or someone else—is so intense, so tender, you don't ever want to revisit it.

Back in Atlanta, I was so relieved to be home that I burst into tears when Pierce and I got into his car to head back to our apartment. Confused, he rubbed my back until I could speak, my sudden emotional breakdown an unwelcome stowaway. He took me home, helped me to bed, and brought me some barbecue, which I left untouched. I was scheduled to return to work immediately, and I moved as if on autopilot for my first two days back. Pierce and I celebrated our third anniversary that week and I told him during dinner I was terrified to go home that night.

"Why are you so scared?" he asked.

I sipped my fancy wine and whispered, "Because I'm afraid I'm going to sleepwalk and kill you."

I'd had intrusive thoughts for years at this point, but none of them had involved the threat of homicide. There had never been a point of such intense despair that I considered taking my own life, but for the first time that thought settled down next to me and made itself at home, a malevolent enemy masquerading as a friend, capable of curing all my pain. It was time to ask for help.

My mother called my boss and told him what was happening, and I drove to my hometown to see her primary-care physician. My great-aunt was there, the woman we affectionately call our matriarch, and for some reason her presence drove home the truth that I was in a bad place. Our aunt is a private woman of few words, but she is practical with her love. When she shows up for you, it's because she knows you need it more than you might expect. As I tearfully detailed what had happened to me in Kenya, and all that had come in the week since my return home, the nurse practitioner took notes and I looked over to see my aunt's eyes filled with tears. In all my life, in all I knew she had endured, I had never once seen that woman cry. It stunned me into silence, her obvious concern for me, and I was momentarily propelled into a place of hope by the reminder that I was loved by a woman like her.

The nurse practitioner asked lots of questions about the medicine I was on, and it became clear that my mental state involved more than my OCD. Unbeknownst to me, the prescription given to me by the health department to prevent malaria, a weekly pill called mefloquine, carries the potential for side effects like insomnia, hallucinations, paranoia, severe anxiety and depression, and suicidal ideation. (This is where I want to scream a bit about pharmaceutical companies and the dark side of capitalism, but I shall resist.) Mefloquine is not recommended for anyone with a history of mental illness or anxiety disorders, and the side effects can last for years or even be permanent. This would have been helpful information for me to know at the health department, but it was not shared with me and, admittedly, I took it on faith that they knew better than I did. Every person on our trip to Kenya had taken a malaria medication, but I was the only one who had selected mefloquine.

When my mother's doctor came in, the nurse practitioner tried to tell him how I needed to stay on the medicine for another week because I could have contracted malaria and not know it. The doctor was a gentle man, soft-spoken and kind, but he held up his hand and cast a stern look in her direction.

"Get her off that medication right now. She doesn't have another week."

I didn't know it then, but eight years later that doctor would help save my life for a second time. God bless modern medicine, to be sure, but God bless doctors who listen more.

I switched over to doxycycline for seven days and felt the effects within twenty-four hours. I became more clear-headed. I could feel the rise and fall of my emotions again, waves of relief and joy and peace. I stayed out of work for the rest of the week, and my coworkers sent me a bouquet of get-well roses. Two weeks later, we celebrated Thanksgiving and all was forgotten. Mostly.

I carried so much shame with me about the trip to Kenya, shame that seemed to have no source and, therefore, no explanation. I recalled many beautiful moments—such as when I first laid eyes on Mount Kilimanjaro, its massive base stretched wide across the horizon, or when a woman from the village blessed a handmade bowl with a prayer of spiritual abundance for me and Pierce—but I beat myself down for what felt like wasted money and wasted time. I couldn't have foreseen what happened to my body, but that didn't stop me from being angry at myself anyway. I'm good at that.

Why didn't you research the medication, Wendi? You're a grown-up. You should know better. Why can't you just relax and stop freaking out? What is wrong with you? This will never get better. You will always be crazy.

Funny how the critical voice in my head often gets the most attention even though I know it's not the voice of God. His is the voice of a loving Father, a Father who disciplines, of course, but who never diminishes. He speaks with purpose and love, and if we feel pain, it's pain that is meant to refine and build us up, not tear us down until we cower in shame. Even now, after decades of loving Jesus, I still have a hard time picking his voice out of the crowd in my head, so comfortable am I with the cacophony of noise that competes for my attention.

You might be tempted to believe that your desperate need for God means something terrible about you, but it actually means something incredible about him. I am forever in awe of a God who makes his strength available to his children, who doesn't separate himself from us but made himself Emmanuel in order to make a way, to ensure that we would never be separated from him again. Our sinful nature is not because our identity as God's good creation has ever changed, but because we believed the lie that said it had. We are tempted to believe it every single day. Praise the Lord, his great love for us means that such lies will never again have the final say.

I want to be a woman who lives in submission to the Holy Spirit. I want to feel the fire of her power course through my veins, filling me with a supernatural strength to walk through this life with a bold and courageous peace. I want to dare to celebrate my weaknesses—even my OCD—because of the unmasking they have done, the clarity they have given me about the actual character of the God I thought I'd known my whole life. I don't know how much mefloquine altered the chemistry in my brain. My mother has long suspected that my current struggles with OCD are a direct result of it, and she might be right. If that's true, it makes me angry. It does not, however, leave me hopeless.

In the fifth chapter of Luke, after the Pharisees had asked Jesus why he ate with tax collectors and sinners, he replied, "It is not the healthy who need a doctor, but the sick. I have not come to call the righteous, but sinners to repentance" (vv. 31–32).

For so long, I thought I was the righteous. I followed the rules. I did the good things. I had no idea that I was chasing the wind when Jesus was there at my side the whole time, inviting me to turn away from all my accolade-seeking and calm down. To rest in him. I didn't want to be a sinner, but I was. I am. It is a good Father, indeed, who won't allow us to continue believing untruths about him. He doesn't have to correct us, but it is his nature. He could leave us where we are, in our self-righteousness, believing we know the answers, but he desires that we come to know him intimately, that we refuse what is less than unity and harmony with him. Such things come at a cost: to our egos, pride, checklists, and rules.

Mefloquine harmed my body, but what its toxicity ultimately laid to waste was my mistaken belief that I needed only to follow the rules—and not the Lord—to lead a moral life. What a hard and holy lesson it has been to learn that God loved me enough to call this sinner to repentance and to show me that he alone can heal. He alone can perfect.

CHAPTER 13

A Place to Hide

For a little over a year my OCD was quiet. It still hovered in the background, but I had grown used to its presence. In late 2012, I had just finished wrapping up the busiest few months I could remember, a short season in which we bought our first house, I took my first novel to a big, intimidating writer's conference, and just before the holidays I completed the most difficult course of my graduate degree. Two weeks before Christmas, as we were beginning to relax into the wonder of the season, I got laid off from my job.

This was not terrible news. The income would be missed, but not the job. I was more than ready to move on.

For a few weeks, I puttered about our house in my pajamas and read *Gone Girl*. I discovered the delight of *Downton Abbey* and locked myself in the office to binge-watch the first three seasons. I considered monetizing my blog and trying to make that a thing, but I had few followers and even less direction. I wanted to write, but about what? I wanted to work for myself, but how?

As all these questions swirled, I sunk deeper into a restless state of uncertainty. I was alone all day, every day (with the exception of Lord and Lady Grantham, obviously), and my mind was working overtime in an attempt to forge the path ahead. One of the guys in our small group did casting for *The Vampire Diaries*—which used to be shot around Atlanta—and I worked as an extra on set a couple of times. (Catch me in the background of season four, episode eighteen!

I'm chillin' at a table behind Nina Dobrev in the restaurant scene. My daughter, Lucy, was there, too, I just didn't know it yet.)

One quiet winter afternoon in January, I sat writing at my desk when an intrusive thought about our neighbor rammed through my brain like a bullet.

What if I walk over there right now and stab someone? You're the only one here. No one can stop you from doing something terrible. Maybe you already have.

What makes these thoughts so hard to work through is that they feel authentic, not just like they could happen but that—somehow, without our knowing—they have. Anyone with an anxiety disorder can tell you this. Intrusive thoughts for someone with OCD have the same physical effects on the body as if you were in real danger, and your hyperactive fight-or-flight mode can't tell the difference. You sweat and you pace. Chills and hot flashes run up and down your spine until you grow nauseated and have to sit down, but you can't sit down because you need to pace. You need to crawl out of your skin and get away from this nightmare or you are going to die.

I jumped out of my seat like someone had poked me with a firebrand, and I howled in agony. "No, no, no," I repeated to myself as I raced to our bedroom, for what I don't know. Solace, maybe, or comfort. I crawled onto the bed and put my hands over my ears, the thought so loud at this point I felt sure I could drown it out somehow. But it was not coming from some external source, at least not one that was visible. It was coming from my own mind, and as I had so many times before, I could not convince myself it had no meaning. How could such a terrible, violent thought mean nothing? Doesn't Scripture tell us "As [a person] thinks in his heart, so is he"? (Prov. 23:7, NKJV). And hadn't these thoughts permeated my heart, filling me up with cruel self-criticism and the conviction that I was lost? Why would I think them if they weren't true?

The brain is a minefield. I can tiptoe around terrible news stories on Twitter and avoid violent content in movies and books, but I cannot always help what headlines happen to pop up on my newsfeed, avoid what trauma is mentioned in a conversation, or stick my head in the sand and never have to confront the awful realities that loom large in our world. I am here, present for such a time as this, and I have to live with the land mines and trust that the skills I've learned in therapy and the graciousness of God will see me through the momentary panic of an intrusive thought.

If you are at all like me, this is what trips us up most when it comes to how we think. We believe that the presence of a thought always has inherent meaning when often it has no meaning at all. When Scripture tells us what we think is who we are, the point is not concerning what random thoughts enter our minds but what thoughts we choose to hold onto, what thoughts we give space, what thoughts we choose to let define us.

For those of us who are privileged to have decent healthcare and community support, we have much more control than we think we do. Our Father has given us free will, and with that comes the opportunity to do hard work, work that requires a lot of help and training and confrontation of difficult beliefs. It is not work we can do alone. It grieves me to think about the people who do not have this kind of community when their thoughts become too burdensome to bear. I have so many resources available to me in the form of healthcare and a generous group of loved ones, and even in my case OCD has been the most painful and life-threatening circumstance I have faced. I cannot imagine the terror of facing it by myself.

Mental health is a tender issue because it causes unnecessary and unjust shame for those who suffer with a chronic condition. This stems from the culture we live in, but it also comes from something deep within, from the sinful nature that lives alongside our inherent goodness as children of God. We are marked by a fallen world, and our enemy knows when we are vulnerable and frightened. He knows that shame perpetuates isolation and isolation perpetuates harm. We hide out because we fear what will happen if we are fully known by those around us, and this leaves our hearts in a dark and fearful place.

In the documentary film *The Heart of Man*, which retells the parable of the Prodigal Son using real-life testimonials from Christians and artistic interpretation of the story, we see a man in intimate relationship with God where together they enjoy all the natural beauty of the world. At some point, the man looks out across the sea to an island that beckons him, an island that represents the places we are tempted to go in this life that promise us fulfillment but will never deliver on that promise. God is playing a violin, and as the man steps closer and closer to the cliff edge, God plays faster and faster, the melody a desperate refrain from a Father to a son. The man jumps into the water and the violin is destroyed, the music that played the soundtrack of their relationship gone. But not forever.

As God has always done, he goes after his son. God finds him chained inside a dark cave, where he has been tortured by the manifestation of his sin and pain. The man thinks he is alone, and then God lights a lamp and we, the audience, see the cave has been filled with other people all along, people the man could not see or hear. Every last one of them is rescued down the path that God had cut through the dense forest long before the man ever stepped foot off the cliff.

It is a film like no other, a gutsy, raw interpretation of the everlasting love we were created with and saved by. I cannot sit through it without tears flowing. It is visceral in its main point, that whether we are chained to a hurtful place by our own sin or by the nature of the world, we are never, ever alone. Isolation is a lie and the chains are already unlocked. There is always someone who has been where we are, who is where we are right now. There is always Someone who has walked the path before us and marked a way through the pain to healing and restoration. There is community and there is God, and we don't have to suffer as though we are trapped inside this dark place with no hope of rescue. The rescue was planned long ago.

● · ● ●● ·

From January 2013 until May of that same year, I could not stay at my house without another person present with me. I didn't have a full-time job anymore, so I was working freelance on resumes and small writing projects to try to supplement Pierce's regular income. I would leave the house each morning with my husband and not return until Pierce came home. I drove all over the city. I tried to escape my brain, but it's a funny thing about brains. They tend to stay with you. I worked in coffee shops and sat in parking lots reading in my car and wrote in corners of Barnes & Noble where I could be surrounded by the books that gave me comfort.

If I had to come home by myself for any reason, I would record a video on my phone as I walked through the house so that I could go back later to reassure myself that nothing bad had happened. This is called reassurance-seeking, and it is a common compulsion for people with OCD. We do not trust our brains, and so we do not trust ourselves.

In certain circumstances, whichever situations tend to trigger our obsessions, we fear that left alone we will lose all control of our faculties and suddenly act out the thoughts that are torturing us against our will. The natural response is to do something that will allow us to prove the thoughts are wrong, but this only tells our brains to work harder at convincing us there is a threat that needs to be addressed. The threat is nonsense, and we know it, but without help we are left with the monumental task of trying to tame the beast ourselves. Sometimes—rarely—this can be done. I've done it, but it is a hell of a lot harder alone and it took weeks, months, and even years longer than it might have if I had known to seek help. These days, I can look at my intrusive thoughts more objectively and say, "Oh, there's my OCD," even when the anxiety spikes and I feel the need to act out a compulsion. But it's a skill I've had to hone for almost a decade, and still there are seasons when the safety of a compulsion wins my favor over the laborious mental work of sitting with the anxiety until it passes.

I hate OCD. It's manipulative and it bullies me to no end if I'm in a tender place. God has heard quite a few colorful phrases from me over the years as I've begged and pleaded for him to remove this thorn from my side. He hasn't chosen to answer my prayers, but he has provided healing. It's a healing that continues, ebbing and flowing, but it is healing regardless.

The very thing that torments me is the offering plate where I've learned to lay down my ego and misconceptions about what rule following has earned me and watch as God takes up my meager donation and uses it for something other than my own personal gain, something richer and far more eternal. A hiding place that does not invite me in to cower from fear and shame but to rest in peace and comfort while the storm rages within my mind and heart. A place where God is unafraid to find and sit with me, as he does for all his children, until we can return once more to the safety of his shore.

14

Not Ready, but Willing

During my hiding-out season, when I refused to be home alone because of my intrusive thoughts, I got pregnant with our daughter, Lucy. Her conception wasn't an accident, but neither was it completely on purpose. When I saw those two pink lines, I looked up at the bathroom ceiling and hissed, "Really, God? Now?!" I had been off birth control for six months and was beginning to wonder if pregnancy was even going to happen. (I know, I know, but I had never tried to get pregnant before, so I was pretty naive about the whole thing.)

Pierce and I had grown tired of all the what-ifs about when to have a baby. We had decided to trust God to make the decision for us because, otherwise, we would have spent another decade waiting on the "right" time to try. After I got laid off, though, and spiraled into perpetual panic mode, I sort of forgot about babies. My brain was fueled by cortisol and caffeine, and tunnel vision kept me zeroed in on the terror of my intrusive thoughts and how I could best avoid them. The idea of pregnancy, and the potential for it, had been steamrolled by OCD. A baby was the furthest thing from my mind, but it was into these months of raging fear and self-criticism that God decided, Yeah, this looks about right.

I was fully aware of what could happen without those baby-blue pills. (Do they make them that color on purpose, I wonder?) I wasn't trying to tempt fate. It was simply that the intensity of my intrusive thoughts left little spare room for anything else in my mind. Walking around, and attempting to function on a normal level, in the body that betrays you is an all-consuming effort, and if I did think of my empty uterus, I thought about it with relief because surely this was not the ideal moment to get pregnant. If the time hadn't been right back when I was healthy and happy (and employed), there was no way my current situation was better. I remained—with God's gentle nudge or my own willful stubbornness, I'm not sure—firm in my conviction that the Lord's timing could be trusted, but that conviction stood strong mostly because I believed I was right and that my dear heavenly Father saw things the same way. I was, after all, a Very Good Christian. God and I were on the same page.

Those two pink lines drew no such conclusion. My HCG levels and an ultrasound agreed. There was a tiny little human in my uterus and I, mental health crisis or no, was going to have a baby.

Five years later, on a hot August morning, I took another pregnancy test and confirmed what I'd already known for days. I was pregnant again, this time with what we found out was our son, Theo. My reaction the second go-round was the opposite of the first. My husband and daughter were busy doing chores while I got ready to go have lunch with some newly graduated students from our church. I took a long, languid shower and caressed my stomach, savoring the knowledge that I was the only person on earth who knew about the tiny life who had just joined our family. There was no panic or fear, just a calm and quiet joy. Then I sat down at the vanity table while Pierce folded laundry and casually informed him, "You might want to get used to all those clothes. There's gonna be a whole lot more of them this time next year." To which he paused with a grin and said, "You're pregnant, aren't you?"

My pregnancies were two distinct ways in which I chose to trust in God. One of them reflected my tiresome need to be right all the time and my longing to be free from playing God. The other represented a more mature faith, the faith of a mother who had walked this road before, who believed more deeply that God is a giver of good gifts and that, sometimes, what we want and what God wants turn out to be the very same things.

In the midst of all my fears, God chose to make me a mother. And when I was brimming with confidence about my ability to carry and raise another child, God said yes again. What those yeses represent is not an affirmation of my goodness or skill over another's, but the eventual willingness of a stubborn heart to yield to the Spirit's gentle—or not-so-gentle—guidance into submission under the lordship of her Creator. Those positive pregnancy tests were evidence of a handful of moments in my life when I can say with certainty that I was not trying to run the show. I was not trying to perform my way into holiness. I was just trying to get out of my own way.

Carrying Lucy pulled me from the river of mental torment that had swept me along for months. I couldn't help but think of her, and as my body shifted to make space for our growing daughter, my mind did too. There simply wasn't enough room for the joy of this baby to live alongside the obsessions that tried to dominate my thoughts. They persisted in their valiant efforts to rob me of my sanity, but the constant change that happens during the ten months of pregnancy (or, in my case, ten-and-a-half months) kept me preoccupied. When we learned we were expecting a Lucy—the name I had chosen for her years before as a little girl obsessed with Lucille Ball—I felt as though I had cheated the system, as if I had succeeded in some daring rebellion against a foreign enemy who wished to see me carted away in chains, forever afraid. Underneath all the questions I'd asked God about whether I should get off birth control had been this refrain, whispered again and again into the corners of my restless soul: "I Am Good." And so he was.

I had wondered for weeks if our second child would be a girl, too, because that seems to be the habit of women in our family. At eleven weeks, I took a blood test that would reveal the baby's sex. I waited impatiently for the results, which came via e-mail one ordinary afternoon while I was homeschooling Lucy. We FaceTimed Pierce while I opened the e-mail, and my eyes dropped right onto the word at the bottom of the paragraph, like a heat-seeking missile. It was a boy, and my heart tumbled around like one of the Magnificent Seven as I imagined who this boy would be. I pictured him tender and generous, like his sister, with a ferocious streak of independence and an inquisitive, sensitive spirit. It felt true. While Lucy had been busy and wild in my womb, forever jamming her elbows into my ribs and causing me to lose my breath, Theo moved like a ballroom dancer, his twirls and dips gentle against my side like the waves of a quiet cove.

We act on faith a whole lot more than we realize. We do this when we pray, laying our troubles and concerns at God's feet in sorrow or gratitude—or both. We do this when we choose to press into our questions, in spite of how they make us feel. We do this when we make love with our partner and expose ourselves to the possibility of parenthood. We do this by the simple act of waking and working each day, believing that somehow all of the mundane, ordinary matters of human life bring glory to God's kingdom. Parenthood has taught me that such mundane, ordinary matters often bring the most glory, just as the messy birth of a lowly Nazarene carpenter introduced an entirely new currency of faith, where give-and-take transactions lose their value in the light of a sacrificial offering that covers all.

I wonder what Mary was thinking when she learned she was going to bear a child, a child not conceived by her husband in a culture that not only devalued women but scorned them, even on good days. Mary was a woman without privilege, but she was not without options. When Gabriel tells her about the boy she has been chosen to carry, a boy who will be known the world over as the Son of God, there is no pause recorded between Gabriel's final statement to Mary and her response.

"'I am the Lord's servant,' Mary answered. 'May your word to me be fulfilled'" (Luke 1:38).

Author and professor Karen Swallow Prior wrote, "Mary's verbal consent to the conception of the Christ child by the Holy Spirit is premised on her informed consent since the words delivered by the angel foretell also the identity and future of the child she will conceive: 'the child to be born will be called holy—the Son of God.' So with Mary's words of 'let it be,' we have what just might be the first recorded instance of verbal consent in human history."

The fact that Mary's consent is included in the narrative should not be glossed over. This is crucial evidence of the kind of God we serve, a God who honors the autonomy he grants his beloved children and does not force his way into their hearts or lives. Mary was chosen to be the mother of the Savior because she was highly favored; there was no question how she would choose to respond to the call of her God. The fact that we get to see her response, that she said yes when she could have very well refused, is more than an example of miraculous faith. It's a testimony of believing God is who he says he is, and believing that he is worthy of our obedience, even when his plans appear nonsensical.

When Mary pondered these things in her heart, did she ever look up at the sky and ask, "Really, God? Now?!" Did she ever want to call Gabriel back and demand a more detailed explanation or even change her mind? I can't help being curious about what we might be missing in the space between the letters, the space where Mary's expectations of her marriage and life with Joseph lived just before Gabriel appeared to her. We, too, live with these spaces. We, too, carry unknowns in our hearts as we walk through lives that unfold before us in ways we couldn't have or didn't plan.

We also carry possibilities, futures that stretch out before us laced with extraordinary hope that our dreams will come to fruition, that our dreams will be approved of by God and, therefore, certain to happen. We so long to be important. We so long to be affirmed. Perhaps it's time we challenge the notion that we aren't valued if our lives take twists and turns off the path we charted for ourselves in young adulthood. Perhaps it's time we be reminded that nothing, "neither death nor life, neither angels nor demons, neither the present nor the future, nor any powers, neither height nor depth, nor anything else in all creation, will be able to separate us from the love of God that is in Christ Jesus our Lord" (Rom. 8:38–39). As my friend Rosalie once told me, God's will is the safest place for us to live. It might not feel safe, especially if your mind is equipped with an overreactive threat detection system, but the security of God's love is an unchangeable reality. Just like the mother of Jesus, we, too, are highly favored. The glorious unknown awaits us if we have the courage to answer, as Mary did, "May your word to me be fulfilled."

The process of waiting for my children to be born renewed my sense of belonging to God and of belonging in this body. For years I had walked through life as though at any second I would unravel, my OCD a shadow that tricked me into distraction and stole many moments of joy. Pregnancy returned that joy to me, and I spent those twenty months carrying my babies in a state of suspended wonder. I wasn't without fear—hmm, what is that like?—but the fear was relegated to its proper station where it could function as it would in any normal brain.

The knowledge that I was a cocreator with Christ in this way served a kind of deep biological need I hadn't been cognizant of until I saw those positive tests. Some sort of gene expression had been flipped on and I was now Mother, a word that contained equal parts of reverence and misgiving within its six simple letters. My fascination often arrived hand in hand with my distaste—I knew birth would be a mess, but who knew pregnancy could be so unsanitary?—and my prayers for our children covered a broad swath of theological ground. I tossed them into the sky like coins into a fountain, my wishes sealed with an intense maternal protectiveness I felt sure God would take into serious account. My understanding of God's love seemed to expand now that I, too, was to become a parent, and, with it, my understanding that there was only so much I'd ever be able to do for my kids. It was power and powerlessness married. It remains that way even now, and I've been told it never ends.

The trust that had been defined as I waited to find out I was pregnant then shifted into confidence the closer I came to birth. But as my children became more developed and nearer to lives not guarded by my flesh and blood, I entered a season of indeterminate faith. It's easy to trust God with our children when they exist only in our minds. It becomes quite a challenge to trust God with them once they're in our arms, out in the cold, lonely world where no one will ever love them the way their mother will. Every new milestone is a cause for both celebration and mourning because every new milestone offers them a whole new world of adventure, and us—their parents—another step closer to the release.

So the cycle continues, a parallel in the way of the Gospel. Our Father creates and watches us grow. With delight for our discoveries, he leads us into unfamiliar territory where we are taught to trust in his guidance. Then, he watches us move into lives of our own, free to step outside of his will but forever covered by the vast expanse of his love.

We are not alone in our expecting and we are not alone in our letting go. This is both the way of motherhood and the way of Emmanuel.

15
Pain and Prejudice

At forty-one weeks and two days pregnant, I was past ready for our son to be born. As I began to lift myself to a sitting position, I felt it: a sharp pop like a glow stick cracked to life inside of me. I cried out in pain and hobbled to the bathroom. My water had broken. Finally.

Within fifteen minutes, my contractions were coming about four minutes apart, and I dialed the midwife on call. The hospital answering service promised to have her call me immediately, but more than a half hour went by with no response. I called again. Another thirty minutes passed.

"You're going to have to call your mom, babe," I told Pierce, a bit frantic. She lived thirty minutes away. He did, and then I heard him tell her we'd "let her know" when she needed to start heading our way.

"No, no, no," I said in disbelief, moaning through a contraction. "What do you mean 'we'll let her know'? She needs to come right now!"

My contractions increased in length and intensity, and still there was no call from the midwife. I breathed in deep lungfuls of air and paced back and forth across the living room, squatting through every contraction and working hard not to tense my body, knowing that the more I tensed, the worse I would feel. I cried out with no concern for our sleeping five-year-old in the next room and rocked from side to side, desperate for relief. Less than two hours after my water had broken, my contractions were coming two minutes apart and I was ready to throat punch someone.

"Wake up Lucy," I said to Pierce. "She can come with us to the hospital. Your mom is just going to have to meet us there."

Pierce rushed to gather our bags, and my cell phone rang. It was my midwife, Angela.

"I'm so sorry," she told me. "They paged the wrong person, twice."

Out of breath, I groaned. "I feel like I need to push."

I heard Angela's sharp intake of air. "Okay. You need to come to the hospital now."

Just as Pierce was about to go wake up Lucy, his mother called. She was a minute down the road. I bent over, hands on knees, by the front door. When she walked in, I said, "Thankyoubye!" and raced to the car. Squatting by the passenger door in the steel-gray light of the early morning, I thought, "Please don't give birth in the car." It was a weekday in Atlanta, the Land of Terrible Traffic, and blessedly we made our way to the hospital just shy of the morning rush. The contractions were so strong and so painful now that all I could do was brace myself against the door and cry out in tears, every bump in the road like a dagger to my lower body.

We got to the hospital at 6:55 a.m. and I made it up the front stairs and into the lobby before I had to lean on Pierce's shoulder and yell through a contraction. The guests waiting to our left leaned over to stare, pure delight on their faces as they watched a mother begin to welcome her child into the world.

I'm so glad you're enjoying this, I wanted to snarl at them.

I was wheeled into the elevator and up to the third floor, where the labor and delivery nurses speedily directed us to a room. It was quiet and bathed in the warm glow of the incubator light, but it was filled with people, Angela among them.

"You need to strip off your shorts after this contraction," she told me in a gentle voice, "so I can check you, okay?"

I nodded, unable to speak.

In the thirty seconds I had to spare between contractions, I took off my shorts and climbed onto the bed. Angela checked me.

"Well, my love," she said with a smile. "You're already dilated past a nine."

"What?!" I shouted, panic rising up in my throat. This was what I'd wanted, an unmedicated delivery with the midwives I trusted in the same hospital where I'd met Lucy for the first time. But now that it was here, all I wanted was the blissed-out nothingness of an epidural. I knew there was no time for such luxuries, and I felt certain I'd die before I dilated another centimeter.

"I have to turn over," I said, sweating and stripping off my shirt. On all fours, I suddenly remembered my husband, who had gone back to park the car and grab our insurance papers. "He's not here," I mumbled into the mattress. "He's going to miss it."

He didn't miss it. Suddenly, Pierce was there next to me, wiping my face with a warm, damp washcloth. "You can do this, wifey," he said, steady as ever.

As if his presence was permission, the need to bear down intensified and I gave myself over to it. I felt vast, as though my whole body had taken up all the space in the room and there was no one else but me and my pain, battling it out to see who would win. I could do nothing but obey the pressure and scream. I heard later that nurses up and down the hallway were chuckling to themselves, my vocalizing a familiar soundtrack over their lives.

"You're almost there," Angela told me as Pierce repeated affirmations in my ear.

"You have to say that to make me feel better," I wept, exhausted.

"No, no, you're almost there," she said again.

"I can't, I can't, I can't."

"You can do this," Pierce repeated. "You're so close."

"I'm gonna die. I can't. This is going to kill me."

An oft-repeated phrase came to me then, the rational side of my brain protecting me just when I needed it most.

When you think you're going to die, it means you're almost done.

"One more push!" Angela exclaimed. "One more push and his head will be out."

Then, like a bodybuilder releasing a primal scream as he lifts the weight of his work in victory, I pushed my son out of my body with a glorious, earsplitting wail.

Panting hard, I asked, "Do you have him?"

"Yes, I'm holding his head right now," Angela replied, a smile in her voice. "One more and he's yours."

Again, I pushed. Again, I screamed.

Then he was there, and I pulled him up from between my legs to my chest, both of us naked and warbling.

"I can't believe it," I sobbed to Pierce, clutching Theo as he cried. "I can't believe I just did that." My water had broken at 4:35 a.m. We arrived at the hospital at 6:55 a.m. Theo was born just seventeen minutes later. Fast and furious, my labor had looked nothing like the quiet, peaceful water birth I'd envisioned for myself over the last forty-one weeks. This was better. This had been an adventure.

My first thought when I saw Theo was how happy I was that he had my Scottish nose, just like his big sister. My second thought was how strange it was to see another child who looked like me and Pierce and, yet, was still so different from Lucy. They shared the same chin, nose, and eye shape, but Theo's lips were thinner, his hair blond at birth where Lucy's had been black. Her full, heart-shaped face was reminiscent of her paternal grandmother, and Theo's long, oval one belonged to his mother and father. It was bewildering to look into the fresh, puffy eyes of another creature we had made and know that he was ours too. I couldn't wait for him to meet Lucy.

My pregnancies had been similar: low risk, past their estimated due dates, tended by midwives I had come to love. My births had only this similarity: vaginal deliveries that resulted in healthy, giant babies, each weighing in at over nine pounds. When Lucy was born, I had gone forty-two weeks and had enough. Hoping a short induction would get me started until my body took over on its own, I agreed to come into the hospital before dawn. Fourteen hours later, after laboring on Pitocin with just a few centimeters of success, I demanded an epidural through tears, feeling very much like a failure.

"Wendi, you're about to have a baby!" the midwife exclaimed. "A baby you carried for over ten months. No matter how she's born, there is no failure in that."

I got the epidural and took an hour-long nap. When I woke up, I was at ten centimeters and ready to push. Lucy had been very comfortable, not content to make her way out into the world just yet, and it took almost two hours of pushing to deliver her. Just before midnight, she made her grand entrance. When I caught that first glimpse of our daughter, held aloft beneath the bright hospital lights like a chunky, delicious beacon of hope, I thought, "There you are!" and began to sob. She was even better than I had imagined.

Neither of my deliveries went according to plan. (This is a surprise to exactly none of you.) And I love to make plans; I live for a new journal and have about five hundred of them tucked away in a purse, on a shelf, under a bench, in my car, or in a drawer. I scribble grocery lists alongside prayers and never write in the same one for more than a couple of days in a row. My journals do not cover linear time, but whatever requires or captures my attention most that day. I make plans for our dinner and I make plans for my writing and I most certainly made plans for the birth of my children. God made other plans.

After Lucy was born, I couldn't tell the story of her birth without feeling the need to add disclaimers about how long I'd labored on Pitocin without an epidural. My closest people were well aware that I'd wanted a water birth, and it was a sincere struggle for me to admit I hadn't been able to go through with it. That I had gotten the painkillers, after all, because my body didn't perform the way I wanted.

"Not because I couldn't hack it, mind you!" I felt the need to say. (But didn't.)

There wasn't a single solitary person who made me feel like an epidural was a failure—either before or after Lucy's birth—but an unmedicated delivery was the expectation I had set for myself. I had written it down in my birth plan. (To which all midwives and nurses say "LOL, cool story, bro.") I had told anyone who'd listen how excited I was about laboring in water and doing this beautiful new thing all on my own. It was a gift being able to carry and bear a child, and I longed to soak up every single lovely, painful second.

And here I was postpartum, allowing an idea of perfection to overshadow the powerful, holy reality that went down in that hospital room. The hard work of labor, medicated or not, that resulted in the birth of my wild girl, my bright and shining star. The weeks of recovery and eight stitches in my vagina and painful nipples and the exquisite wonder of her newborn smell as I nursed her to sleep. The birth plan had changed, but the truth about what she was—what we had done together—had not.

The temptation to feel as if Theo's birth redeemed my perceived failure the first time around came on strong a few days after he was born. And, to be honest, I had to fight it. The words of my midwife echoed in my head throughout my second pregnancy: "No matter how this baby is born, there is no failure in that." As I went past my due date again, I had grown more anxious in anticipation of a second induction, a second epidural. I was determined to do this my way. And I had. Kind of.

Unmedicated birth had certainly shown me the power of womanhood, had offered me a connection to all the women of the past who bore down in cottages and forests, in temples and palaces, and gave me a glimpse of the universality of birth, how it cares not one iota about who you are. The bloody, messy beauty of the experience is its hallmark, whether you have given birth once or five times, whether you are a queen in a castle or a suburban mom in a split-level.

Unmedicated birth also revealed my own prejudice. There were dozens of questions, and a bit of side-eye, from well-meaning family and friends who were curious about my departure from what they viewed as a safe and normal birth, but once they understood why I felt so strongly about it, they supported me. As I labored with Theo and cried out in pain, I felt a profound mixture of gratitude and empathy with my fellow women. Birth without fear? That looks different for me than it might look for someone else. An epidural, a failure? Praise the good Lord above for medicine that lets women deliver their children without being forced to experience pain they don't want to or can't endure, because the pain is coming later regardless. (As are the mesh underwear—get ready for those beauties!) There is no such thing as the easy way out. This shit is tough.

It was a lie that my unmedicated second birth had redeemed my medicated first. The only thing that needed redemption was my faulty perspective. When I settled onto that hospital bed with Theo in my arms, I looked at Pierce and said, "That was incredible. And I never, ever want to do it again." In the weeks that followed, I gained a new sense of awe, and sadness, as I imagined women being forced to give birth year after year, with no hope of painkillers or birth control pills to reduce their pain or potential suffering. My unmedicated labor had simultaneously boosted my long-held belief that women can do this without intervention and also strengthened my resolve that they should be presented with options, not forced into thinking they have no choice about what kind of delivery is available to them. Birth is universal, but women are unique in their needs and wants.

Sometimes we get what we're hoping for and it turns out to be an unexpected saving grace. Rather than the redemption we thought we needed, we gain open eyes and softened hearts. We learn to set our expectations aside for the sake of solidarity with others because the need to perform in even our most intimate moments runs deep, but it will never give us more space at the table. It will only prevent us from sitting down together and sharing our stories.

Women don't need another reminder that they have more to prove. This is the reality we live with regardless of whether or not we are mothers. In the birthing room we have an opportunity to watch God move among us in the Spirit of unity, where our deepest longings are met with honor and our deepest fears are met with compassion. Defining us by the way in which we birthed our children is to identify us according to what we do, not who we are, and to diminish us as cocreators with Christ and children of the living God.

We can carry our desires about what we need for childbearing, about what is good for our particular circumstance, and clasp hands in solidarity with another woman as she does the same. God is present in both. He is present in all.

Part Four

Receiving Holy

CHAPTER **16**

Listening in the Darkness

I felt so *normal*. What a relief. Convinced I would need to fight my emotions after delivering our son, I found it a pleasant surprise to discover the quiet inside my mind and the peace inside my heart.

My newborn son was tucked inside my hospital gown, asleep on my chest with nothing but a palm-sized diaper on, and the three of us—me, my husband, and Theo—were basking in the warm glow of our new normal. My body was tender from labor, and the discomfort of giant ice pads and half-open hospital gowns put a slight damper on things, but overall, I was at ease. I was clear-headed and calm, eager for Lucy to meet her baby brother. Even Pierce commented on my demeanor.

"You seem so back-to-normal," he told me. "Like, 'I just had a baby. No big deal!'"

I laughed, triumphant. It was an unexpected benefit to an unmedicated delivery, and his comment matched my thoughts. Even I was a bit shocked that I wasn't more weepy or discombobulated.

We enjoyed a long, lazy morning together in our hospital room before my mother and mother-in-law called to tell us they were bringing Lucy over to see Theo. The bright, spring sun cast rays of warmth across my body, and I tilted my chin to kiss our son's head a hundred times as he dozed. He had his father's slender, elegant fingers, and I picked up his little hand to marvel at the intricacy of his form. My thoughts were fixed on this heavenly creature, and I knew no anxiety, no intrusive thoughts. Just peace.

Lucy entered the room with her grandmothers and showed us all the sweet drawings she had made for Theo, including a lovely rendition of a baby-blue birthday cake. She was shy and uncertain, eager to be near her new little brother but not close enough to touch him.

"He's pink," she noted, incredulous and a bit wary.

My mother knew the trick. She took Theo from Pierce and sat on the end of the bed, beckoning Lucy to come over and look.

"How many fingers can you see? Do you think he has all ten?" she asked, very serious. Lucy peered over the blanket as my mother unwrapped his swaddle. She couldn't resist a pop quiz. I watched as she counted to herself.

"He does!" she exclaimed, and then moved in closer. More questions followed, and soon Lucy was up on the bed, asking to hold her brother for the first time. We showed her how to support his head, and a wild collection of emotions rose in my throat, robbing me of words. People had told me this moment would be a good one, and they had been right. My entire world, wrapped up in flesh and bone, was there in front of me, and I was happy.

After a hospital lunch for me and some Chick-fil-A for Pierce, we made plans to get our dog, Bella, a spot at the doggy daycare that afternoon since we would be spending the night in the hospital.

"I think it's about time for your mom to take Lucy home, so I'm just going to go on and get Bella, too, so you can sleep," Pierce said. "Is that okay?"

An image came to me then, unbidden and unwanted, as though someone had spliced a violent photo into an otherwise delightful film: an image of me alone in the room with our newborn son, doing something awful. My OCD interrupted a happy, joyful narrative because that's how anxiety operates. It's really good at making us doubt what we know to be true, especially when our lives—and our hormones—are at peak transition.

I swallowed hard as a shot of adrenaline pulsed through my body. "Please don't," I whispered, my eyes wide. Pierce nodded, understanding. He looked back at me with sympathetic eyes and squeezed my hand.

"Okay," he said. My mother and mother-in-law agreed to hang out while Pierce took care of Bella. I let them take turns holding their new grandson, and my heart ached with sorrow and fear. Our beloved boy wasn't even a day old yet, and I was already terrified to be alone with him. My OCD had zeroed in on a new vulnerability within me and gone right for the jugular.

That night, we barely slept more than an hour. Theo was fussy and unable to rest, so Pierce and I took shifts holding him while the other tried to get some shut-eye. Theo was nursing constantly, and I hated being awake with him alone. That first intrusive thought had triggered a flood of them, and I was suddenly in hell. All night, as Theo cried and nursed, I fixed my hands on the parts of his body I deemed safe, like his upper back and legs. I avoided his bottom and made Pierce change his diaper. My brain was screaming at me, torturing me with images of harm, pulling content from every horrible news report I'd ever seen or read.

"You are gonna do that," it accused me. "You're going to hurt your son. Why else would you think of something like that? Those other people did it, those people you heard about. They were normal once, too, and then they turned evil. That's what you're going to do. You're going to abuse your son. You're going to kill him if you get the chance. It's only a matter of time."

Those are just thoughts, I repeated quietly to myself as I bounced Theo in my arms, both of us teary and exhausted. *God made me his mother and I am good.* It's a timeless refrain spoken from every mother's lips as she wonders if she is really capable of loving her child well.

I didn't realize it yet, but postpartum depression had set in, and hard, given my already present OCD.

After we got home from the hospital, we found out that Theo was tongue-tied and could not effectively pull milk from my breast, hence his constant fussiness. I began pumping every two hours to feed him and would get just enough for one feeding before I'd have to go pump again to prep for the next. My days became an endless cycle of *pump, feed, rock, maybe shower or brush my teeth, pump, feed, did you touch him the wrong way when you changed his diaper? pump, feed, change, oh yeah! Lucy needs me too, pump, feed, shove some food in my mouth, pump, feed, don't hurt your son.*

By the end of the first week, after the visitors had come and gone and it was just the four of us at home, I'd sunk deep into the shadows of myself. I hovered on the edge of hysteria and a vast ocean of nothing, always at risk of sobbing uncontrollably or just staring across the room, the obsessions turning me almost catatonic with fear. My joy was manufactured for the sake of our daughter, who was having to adjust to so many big changes already, but there was no now, no present. There was only the future—a future where I was locked up in prison or a mental hospital, my children without their mother and, worse, their mother a monster. Every second that passed brought me closer to the day Pierce was scheduled to go back to work, and with those seconds I grew more and more depressed. I could not escape the darkness. It fed on my mind and my soul and was never satiated.

My only reprieve was sleep. At nine o'clock every night, after the kids were in bed, I passed out on the couch to the sound of Leslie

Knope's incessant chatter on *Parks and Recreation*. If I got lucky and Theo slept until three the next morning, I'd be grateful that I got six hours of rest because once I was awake, the intrusive thoughts would begin anew. I'd sweat through the sheets, my heart and mind racing, and have to get out of bed and race to our back porch. There, with a fresh cup of coffee in hand—my one guaranteed comfort—I'd stare up at the sky and weep, bereft of faith. God had disappeared and left me alone in despair. God didn't even exist anymore. Prayers were whispered and curses were howled, but none of it mattered. God was gone, and all my hope had gone with him.

● · · ●●●   ·

In early 2013, during my hiding-out season, it was determined that I was in serious need of prayer, so I sent my small group a short e-mail telling them that I was in a poor mental state and could really use their support. We were a lively group of women, some of whom I'd known for years and some who were still virtual strangers, but they were a secure landing place for me. At our meeting the previous Thursday, I'd talked to them about my OCD in bits and pieces, but this e-mail was my first real cry for help.

The next day, I arrived home from a full day of aimless driving and avoidance and sat in my car waiting for Pierce to pull up so I could go in without being alone. Through the raindrops pelting my windshield, I saw a gorgeous bouquet of sunflowers, my favorite, sitting by the front door—wilted, but still bright enough to pierce the gray afternoon gloom. I ran inside and plucked the card from the leaves. It was from one of the women in my small group. We had talked a few days before about our favorite flowers, and she had remembered mine. (I would come to learn over the years that this woman is a rare human being, her heart a deep reservoir of generosity and love.) The gentle encouragement from a new friend boosted my spirits. I texted her to say thanks and put the bouquet on our dining-room table.

On Tuesday, I came home to a second bouquet, this time tulips from another small-group member. On Wednesday, another bouquet. My e-mail had stirred my friends to action, and thanks to a message sent to the group without my knowledge, my dining room table was soon laden with a dozen varieties of flowers, each one of them an offering of peace for my weary soul, a reminder that I was held up and covered by the love of dear friends.

Six years later, our small group had experienced one transition after another, and by the grace of God we had remained an intimate family. Women joined for community and a safe place to ask hard questions and, later, they left for jobs and grad school and babies. We celebrated victories and grieved losses and made it a point to talk and laugh about stuff no one ever discusses in pews. Pierce and I loved our Big Church, but those women were my little church, my Thursday church, the ones who walked with me through the most difficult times of my life and cheered for me even when I was stumbling around in the dark.

In those early postpartum days after the birth of my son, I felt the prayers of my Thursday church even when I did not feel God. And I was bombarded by texts and phone calls from other beloved women, some speaking to my specific need and some just letting me know I was on their minds. A candle arrived in the mail from my longtime bestie with a message of love and hope printed on the lid: "You are strong. You are amazing, Theo and Lucy's superhero. Remember." I cried over the words of my loved ones because as much as they continued to carry me across the chasm of my pain, I felt sure I was not worthy of their love. A tender palm on my cheek or a worried brow in my direction sent shockwaves of grief into my heart over what I believed would be lost in the battle of my mind. I had all I'd ever wanted, except for peace, and I mourned as if it had all been burned to ashes.

Those back porch coffee sessions became a daily ritual. As my family slept soundly in the house, I'd tiptoe through the kitchen and out the back door where I'd collapse in exhaustion on the steps, shaking with anxiety.

"Where are you, God?" I demanded of the sky. I remembered my homeschool days out there with Lucy, running around in the grass, searching the branches above for male cardinals, their breasts like drops of red paint among the canvas of green and brown. We had memorized their call—"pur-ty, pur-ty, pur-ty"—but the cardinals were quiet now. Like God. The silence screamed back at me.

"You gave me this boy," I hissed through tears, vacillating between anger and sorrow. "You gave me this life and I trusted you. Now make it right, okay? Please, God. Please. You better make this right."

The silence wore on, but I kept coming back to it because I didn't know another way. I had seen God at work in my life again and again, had crossed deep valleys to reach mountains of joy, and though my spirit grieved, it also anchored me to plain old stubborn faith. The need to be right, to see God return, shoved through the silence and sat down with me like a church mother taking her seat in the front row. My brain told me depression would stretch into eternity; my spirit told me to just take a damn shower.

People were afraid. I could see it all over their faces, and I heaped shame on myself for frightening them. My children needed a healthy mother. My husband deserved a sane wife. My family and friends wouldn't be able to keep up with this illness for long. At some point, it would consume me and them along with it.

Depression assumes its importance like a dictator who refuses to hear reason. It wants power and takes it by force. Mothers who suffer with depression feel doubly accosted because the vast, empty nothing steals even their most potent joy, the joy of loving and being loved by their children. It is a sinister, quiet terror, and the stealth of the disease, especially for postpartum women who are already experiencing so much transition, is what makes it so dangerous.

When Pierce went back to work, I lasted about three hours at home alone with my children before the bully in my brain had me convinced I was about to fall apart. The combination of constant anxiety and the heavy weight of depression worked in tandem to secure my need for companionship, and I was grateful to have loved ones to whom we could turn for help.

A dear friend of mine since our Bible study days in college spent two days with me just to be present while Pierce was at work. She helped clean the house and entertain my daughter and remind me that I was still a functioning human being capable of more than what this illness had spoken over me. One morning, as I sat nursing on the couch in desperate need of a meal and some fresh clothes, my friend said, "Go on and take a shower. I'll take care of things out here." While I stood under the hot water, feeling hollow as a shell, unable to cry anymore, an arm shot out from behind the curtain and waved a hot mug of coffee back and forth, an offering of peace and love.

"A little coffee in the shower, my dear?" she crooned. As I reached out and took the mug, laughter caught in my throat. "There's nothing better when you're feeling down." When you have no idea what to do next, let your friends be your guide. They'll give you exactly what you didn't know you needed.

For weeks, I wrestled with what I knew to be true of God and the utter emptiness I felt inside. I had no motivation to do anything other than get through the day so I could go back to sleep, but I knew the time was coming when a choice would have to be made. I only hoped I'd have the courage to step forward when there was no guarantee my mental health would ever improve.

What if God was silent forever? What then?

"God is still here, Wendi," my friend assured me later, after she had returned home. I had not improved since that coffee in the shower; in fact, I was perilously close to becoming a postpartum statistic, and I was angry with the God who had always loved me so well. This depression, these obsessions and compulsions, could not be love. Love doesn't wound. Love doesn't feed off fear. Love doesn't condemn your every imperfect thought and sentence you to a lifetime of mental hell.

When you grow up believing your correct behavior earns a matched response from God, tragedy must be a result of your own failure to perform well. I begged God to remove my mental illness, to heal me once and for all. I questioned why it remains even after I'd done the hard work of healing.

Hasn't it taught me what it needed to, Lord? How much more are you going to ask of me?

We had asked God for a child, and he had given him to us: Theodore, whose very name means "gift of God." So where was God in this pain? Why give us a son if he would soon be without a mother to raise him?

I don't believe God orchestrates trauma, but it's clear that he allows it. It makes sense that a Creator who is Love will allow love without limits, and so it follows that there is the potential for pain without limits too. They are partners together in this life, and the one increases the potency of the other. I lived this during my labors, and I lived it afterward too.

My OCD amped up because I had experienced a massive life change, and that life change brought with it a cascade of hormonal upheaval that invited anxiety's dearest friend, depression, to come along for the ride. Atop these physical and mental tribulations perched my ever-present fear that I would never recover spiritually, and this struck me as an especially cruel threat. I had walked with God for a lifetime, and I felt tempted to abandon him because I suspected that he had abandoned me. But fear prevented me. Once again, I tried to be faithful because I was afraid of what unfaithfulness meant. Perfectionism was wound intricately together with my despair, and I could escape neither. I would either live through this trial and be free, or I would take my own life in an arresting display of sorrow. It would be perfection or total destruction, but there would not be, and could not be, a middle ground.

I was not alone in this experience, but pain is such that while others can walk with us in it, we must live through it on our own. There is no one who can survive depression for us. And so, miracle of miracles, we press our hands to our hearts and feel the beats continue. We nurse our babies. We change another diaper. We eat another meal. We move, even if the effort it takes is monumental. We let our bodies take the lead in keeping us alive because they will not go without a fight. They are persistent in their need to survive, and this is the endowment of our God, who planned a resurrection and carried out an impossible fulfillment of life after death. When our minds are dying, somehow our bodies press on, however feeble. This, too, is love.

"Maybe," my friend encouraged me, "it isn't that God is silent. Maybe he's just talking to you in a whole new way."

Maybe, just maybe, he is louder than ever before.

Lord, give me ears to hear.

CHAPTER 17

Two True Things

I have often wondered what it would be like to have no religion. God has been a part of my vocabulary from the moment I entered the world, and I have no concept of what life is like without him. At least, until recently.

Years ago, when I was a young adult mourning the break-up of a romantic relationship, my mother told me that sadness would one day give way to anger, which would ultimately become indifference. Then, she said, I would be okay. Then, I would be over it. My mother was right, as she has often been. I was sad, and then I was mad, and then, as if by magic, I was unbothered. I moved on and fell in love again and the world kept turning.

My mornings on the back porch with God felt a little like that. I was in the trenches, sometimes unable to do much more than whisper through tears. Other times, I fumed through bouts of intense fury with God. The final step was indifference, and I didn't want to become indifferent about Jesus. He was my lifelong friend, but whether I begged or cursed God, that seemed to be his response to me. Indifference to my tears, indifference to my pain, and—worst of all—indifference to what this would do to my family and children should it continue.

About a month after Theo was born, we established a kind of malleable summer routine where Lucy, who had never spent an entire day away from me unless it was to go on vacation with her grandparents, attended an all-day church camp while I took Theo to my mother-in-law's house. This was a painful adjustment for a number of reasons, not least of which is that my daughter had already endured a massive transition to big sister and we had next to zero time to prep her for the shift from being at home all day with me to being at a strange, new summer camp from eight to five with people she had never met. There is only so much change a kid can go through before they start to crack, and the guilt I felt about not being able to hold up my end of the bargain—not being able to be at home alone with my children—intensified as my daughter struggled to adjust.

I sought counseling and found a therapist fast with the help of my Thursday church. My insurance didn't cover the cost, so we did our best to make it work, but the unexpected expense of summer camp and talk therapy added to my stressors. Even with the resources we have under private insurance, trying to find an appropriate doctor so I could begin medication was an absurd ordeal. I called number after number in our network, just to be told I had to enroll in a whole counseling program in order to be seen, or that such-and-such doctor wasn't actually in network, or that an initial consultation would cost almost four hundred dollars.

"It's a good thing I'm not suicidal," I said to my husband one afternoon in a terrible attempt at a joke. He didn't think it was funny.

My obsessions had intensified with every new obstacle to healing, and I was now at the point where even driving in the car with my son would send my mind tumbling over one harm thought after another. On the way to my mother-in-law's house each morning, I would grip the steering wheel and try not to move my hands.

"You're not reaching back there, Wendi," I'd assure myself again and again. "Your son is fine and you are not hurting him. You couldn't even reach him unless you leaned over the seat. See your hands? They're on the steering wheel. Check the clock. See the time. Then you can recall exactly what you were doing when you try to remember this later."

Again and again, I would perform this compulsion to reassure myself. I would work to memorize the order of every song that played on the radio while we drove the half hour to my in-laws', and after we'd arrive I would escape to another room alone so I could try to remember every single time I'd moved my hands to change gear or use the turn signal.

"Oh God," I'd cry in anguish, bent over in a ball on the floor. "But what about that thirty-second block of time between when I turned and when I stopped at that stoplight? What song was playing then? I can't remember! What was I doing then? Where were my hands? What if I hurt my son but don't have any memory of it?"

OCD's most powerful tool is uncertainty. People who suffer from the disorder cannot abide uncertainty, because it leaves too many holes, too many unknowns, from which our minds can terrorize us with all sorts of imaginary scenarios. We know what is true, but the what-ifs play on our fears, on what we love most in all the world. The very thought of harming my son sent me into distress. This was evidence of how far away I was from acting on my obsessions, but it didn't matter. I had built a habit of performing compulsions to reduce my anxiety, and my brain had been trained to think those compulsions were necessary safeguards against the perceived risk. It was a cycle that would never end unless I took drastic action to make it stop. Increasingly, my mind would turn to suicide as the only way to ensure all of this would end.

"If something happens to me," I said to Pierce one morning as I headed out the door, "please give my journals to the kids."

Pierce shook his head, his expression grave. "Babe, that's not going to happen. This is going to get better."

I brushed tears from my cheeks and took a deep, shuddering breath. "Just tell them I'm sorry and I love them and that this wasn't their fault, okay? Please. Promise me you'll tell them."

"I'm not going to tell them because you're not going anywhere," Pierce replied, his fear coming out like anger. "Don't say things like that."

Still, thoughts of suicide lingered. I would reach the point of mental anguish where I had no faith that my health would improve, and the enemy would whisper, "There's always a way out." It was a sinister temptation, and there were moments when I felt relief at the idea that I had options. It was a twisted, toxic hope. It was no hope at all.

Then I would picture my daughter's beautiful face, tears streaked down her cheeks, and feel her grief-shattered heart when she learned that her mother had chosen to leave her behind. And I would take another breath.

I became obsessed with knowing the answers, with understanding my mental illness even though my therapist had already read the definition of Obsessive Compulsive Disorder in the Diagnostic Statistical Manual, or DSM.

"You are aware of what is true," she would encourage me. "You know what year it is, how old you are. You aren't having hallucinations, you don't have schizophrenia, and you fit every single descriptor for OCD. You aren't going to suddenly act in a way that is contrary to your nature, Wendi. Your brain is simply in overdrive, and we are going to work to put it back in the proper gear."

I was the textbook version of an OCD sufferer. I had finally reached some level of perfection after all.

But I needed to know more. I needed to understand the difference between a technical glitch in my prefrontal cortex and a depraved mind. This distraction felt like progress, but it was just another compulsion. One afternoon, as Theo napped downstairs with his grandmother, I spent an hour online researching what various faith communities theorized about the eternal consequences of suicide. Would God have compassion on my broken heart, or would he turn his face from me? I couldn't know, but I tried to find out. Another compulsion.

The list continued to grow, and the compulsions ate away at all my spare time and mental strength. My therapist and I had a lot of work to do, but before I could begin to tackle the hard work of breaking old, familiar neural pathways, I needed to get myself on stable ground.

I gave up trying to find a practice in my network and called my mom's doctor again, the same one who had seen me after my trip to Kenya eight years earlier. The receptionist told me he wasn't seeing new patients until November. It was June.

"Listen," I demanded in a shaky voice. "I am telling you that this is desperate. I just had a baby and I have OCD and depression. If you can't get me in to see someone today, I have no idea what's going to happen to me."

At three o'clock that afternoon, I drove an hour back to my hometown and met my older sister at the doctor's to see the physician's assistant who was able to fit me in. After an hour-long wait, I was taken back to the exam room. When the door opened a few minutes later, it wasn't the physician's assistant who walked in but my mother's doctor.

He sat with me until past closing time. He asked questions, took notes, and explained all the medications available to me in detail. He was a calm, clear lake under a cloudless blue sky: safe, trustworthy, and full of peace. My big sister held my hand and asked the questions I forgot to ask, and when the doctor got up to leave the room, he put his hand on mine and pressed with a gentleness that spoke volumes. "I'm so sorry this is happening to you," he said with tired eyes. "You'll be in my prayers every day."

Things got worse before they got better. By my next therapy appointment, the placebo effect of the antidepression medication had worn off and my therapist nearly called 911. My sister was in the lobby waiting for me. Before we left, my therapist told her I wasn't allowed to be on my own for at least a week. So my sister packed up her life and parked it on my couch for a while. Every day, we got up and took care of the kids. She helped us keep our schedule as simple and as normal as possible for the sake of all our sanity while I got help. On the Friday she was due to go home, I asked her to leave me alone with my son.

"Just go to the coffee shop down the road for an hour," I told her. My flight or fight response was alive and kicking, but I reminded myself that I had been here before. I had done this and done it well. It could be done again. "He's asleep right now and if I need you, I'll text you immediately."

This was my first attempt at resisting a compulsion. As soon as my sister walked out the door, my brain dumped a shitload of chemicals into my body in response to what it perceived as a threat to our well-being.

Run away, OCD insisted. This is not safe.

"Shut the hell up," I said out loud to my kitchen. I cleaned and started the dishes and forced myself to go into the bedroom to check on Theo while he slept. I watched over him with tears in my eyes as his little chest rose and fell, both terrified out of my mind and ecstatic that I was here with him, alone, for the first time since he was born. I made it the full hour without a panic attack. In fact, the thrill of a tiny step forward felt like a gold medal, and I could almost feel my brain building new pathways in response.

Every week, I went to therapy. We talked about God and perfectionism and the extremes in which I had lived for as long as I could remember. My life was a world of black and white, right and wrong, and OCD had encouraged me to fear what lived in the middle of those extremes. This, too, had been the way of my faith. I already questioned those gray areas where the rules I lived by didn't add up for me or others I knew, but it was rare that I ventured into them. Faith had been an equation with a single clear solution for every circumstance, and whenever I'd felt a curious tug in a gentler direction, I never trusted it. It was for the lukewarm, those gray areas, and I would soldier on until I discovered what appeared to be the right answers.

My therapist taught me, little by little, that more than one thing can be true at a time. This is a common sentiment, and for good reason, but she made it fresh and alive for me again. God gave us two hands so we can carry two truths together. I can have OCD and still be a strong, healthy mother, a good wife. I can love God with my whole heart and still be angry with him. I can have been given an idyllic childhood, full of whimsy and love, and still bear wounds from it that need to be processed.

Our world, and our faith, is a complex, diverse, messy, wonderful creation. It is full of contradictions and a whole host of unknowns. But we can know Jesus. When all appears uncertain, he remains. He holds us together, with hands that bear the scars of his love so that even in doubt, even in suffering, we are secure. We can fight over all the details and live in the extremes, battling for perfection, or we can submit ourselves to the authority of Jesus and discover the easy burden of a holy, human God. We are positioned to embody all the mercy we've been given so that the light of the Good News will burn for others to come up underneath its warmth and find a place of refuge. Yes, we will bear our crosses, but we need not crucify ourselves on them. Jesus took care of that, and when we strive to live out perfect faith by punishing ourselves for all we cannot achieve, we tell the Great I Am that he is not quite great enough.

We are all of us wandering souls on a quest for home. We have a restless longing for more and a need to quench that desire, so we look for it in performance, in affirmation, in achievement. In the rules that guide our faith so we can hold up our lives as examples of goodness.

The hard truth is the only goodness we can claim is the goodness of Jesus Christ, who formed us and continues to shape us, more and more, into people like him the longer we trust in his authority. As I learn how to live well with a mental health disorder, with a mind on 24/7 alert for extremes, I come to understand the need for nuance in faith, the need to hold space in our hands for more than one true thing at a time.

In Ephesians, Paul tells the young church there: "Watch what God does, and then you do it, like children who learn proper behavior from their parents. Mostly what God does is love you. Keep company with him and learn a life of love" (5:1, MSG).

Mostly what God does, Paul tells us, is love us. Our job is to love like that, in the extravagant way of the cross. The other stuff, the rules and restrictions, are opportunities for conversation, curiosity, and debate. They offer wisdom and guidance in uncertain times, and encouragement when we aren't sure how to continue on the path.

If we want to get to the end of our lives and stand justified in the presence of Jesus, then our primary job is not perfect theology but to "keep company with him and learn a life of love."

This is the life I long for, a holy life modeled by the King who redeemed my broken mind and broken heart and set my feet on solid ground. I want no more promises of perfection from the televangelist in my mind, no more obstacle courses designed to trip me up over a particular exegesis, no more lies from OCD that say if I don't keep a viselike grip on every behavior, then I will default to evil.

I am a sinner, and God is good. And since God is good and I am his beloved daughter, then so am I. Two things, both true, at the same time.

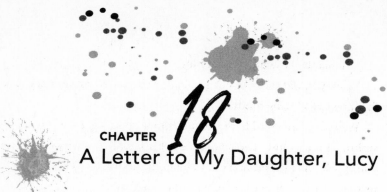

CHAPTER 18

A Letter to My Daughter, Lucy

Dear Lucy,

I'm sitting on the couch next to our Christmas tree and remembering this time last year. I was pregnant with your little brother, about four months in, and you had asked me a dozen times when you'd be able to feel him kick.

"He has to grow bigger before you can feel him," I'd say. You were a little jealous that I could already, but I tried to bring you into the experience as much as possible. We checked my pregnancy apps every week to see how big he'd grown, and I took that time to go ahead and talk to you about how babies are made, seeing as how your brother's existence had already charted curious new paths for your little mind. You were unfazed by the details. You even watched birthing videos with me and never grimaced once. You were dazzled and sometimes confused, which was a huge win as far as I was concerned. Never disgusted. Never scared. (You're way ahead of the curve, baby girl.)

Two weeks before Christmas, we sat down on the couch together, just me and you, after a long day stuck in the car. I pulled out brother's ultrasound photos from that afternoon, and we talked about how cute he looked, how we thought he was going to have our nose. Then you put your hand on my belly and Theo kicked you. I felt it from the inside and you felt it from the outside, and for just a moment we were all connected. You gasped with delight and your eyes widened over an open-mouthed grin.

"Mama, he kicked me! I felt him!"

"I know! I did too! Oh my gosh, you were the first one, Lucy. The first one to feel baby brother!"

Well, that was it. There was nothing else to be done. You were smitten and proud, and everyone who had the fortune to cross your path for the next few weeks heard about your early Christmas present. I can tell you as your mother that this felt ordained from heaven. Every parent wants their babies to be best friends, and the truth is I was a little nervous. You had been an only child for five years, almost six by the time brother was born, and we weren't sure how you'd adjust.

It took some time once he was born, but you did adjust. And I am still so proud of you. This year has offered you one challenge after another, and with each one you continue to amaze—but never surprise—me. There were some weeks when our hearts were broken; you didn't understand why you had to go to all-day summer camp and be away from me, and I couldn't tell you much beyond how we wanted you to have some place to go and have fun while we did all the hard parent stuff. It gutted me to leave you behind, to have to walk away from you while you cried, because I needed to go to therapy so that you would still have a mom to come home to at night. I thought about you all day and prayed for you constantly. I crept into your room while you slept and told God he had better take good care of you, that he had better send you kind friends and help you forget, just for a few hours, how much you missed me. We were best buddies, you and I, and it was time for us to weather our first big storm together. This was the hardest thing I've ever done in my life.

One afternoon, when we were headed home, I told you that I was sick and that part of why you'd had to go to summer camp was so that I could talk to someone and see a doctor. I told you about hormones and how some moms feel really sad after having a baby, even though they are so happy about being a mother. I told you my brain works a little differently and that I was sorry things had been tough since brother was born. I had wanted us to be together every day, as I had planned, and I explained how these changes sometimes made me even sadder.

Then, Lucy, you said something I had told you a hundred times, something I learned from the author John Steinbeck, and those few words filled my sorrowful heart with hope.

"I know it's not the same as you wanted," you told me from the back seat. "But remember? Things don't have to be perfect to be good."

How easily we forget the lessons we've learned. This is the beauty of loving people, my sweet girl. What God has taught us will always come back through the wise counsel of trusted friends, family, and daughters. What I teach you will eventually become a lesson I must learn again, and so it is a precious privilege to be in this relationship with you. People will let us down and sometimes they will even betray us, but the Lord will never stop teaching us the truth about himself. God will never leave us in our grief or confusion, for he has given us a Helper who offers clarity to muddled minds. He speaks through the mouths of children to moms who have lost their courage. He gives us glimpses of himself in the people we love, for they, too, bear the *imago Dei*. In Jesus, we can know each other, and in each other we can know him.

I could talk more about how I lived through the trauma of postpartum depression and the ensuing obsessions and compulsions that dominated my time in that season, but while those difficulties loomed large then, I see now that they were symptoms of another, deeper issue.

You see, Lucy, your mother is a perfectionist. You might not understand what that word means right now, but I am almost certain you understand what it looks like. I'm hard on myself and I hate to make mistakes. I work with great diligence to guard myself against my own humanity, and I'm sure you've seen this in action. While I'm busy encouraging you with affirmations like the one above, my desire to be good drives me so hard I cannot even bear the simplest of personal slip-ups.

"Fix it, fix it, fix it," demands my inner critic.

"Fix what?" you might ask.

Anything. Everything. A hair out of place or a broken heart.

Can I tell you a lesson I've learned? I can see you placating me with a smile right now. Whenever I turn down the music in the car to answer your questions, you know a lesson is coming. It's annoying, I know, but these conversations are deposits for your future. I have to believe they'll prove useful to you in a desperate moment. Motherhood is a constant act of faith.

But back to the lesson. Right.

I've learned, Lucy, that I am not God. (Shocker, I know.) When I fear the loss of control, what I really fear is the loss of my identity, the identity I embraced from a faith culture that steered me with good intentions but ultimately navigated me to a place where God is good only if we are good.

Who wants to love a God like that? Who wants to love a parent like that?

If being your mother has taught me anything, it's that you could burn the world to ashes and I would love you still. You could hate me and I would embrace you anyway. There is no affection in this imperfect mother's heart that would diminish should you abandon the path we've taught you to walk. I wish I could take credit for such love, but I cannot. It was imprinted on my soul by Love Itself (God!) and, as such, finds its source there. There is no failure that can drain the source, nor any success that can improve it. It is unchangeable and eternal. It remains, always, exactly as we hope it will.

Perfection will greet you with a smile and say, "Job well done," if you have lived up to its standards. If not, expect a frown and a cold shoulder.

God greets us with a race across the field, arms outstretched regardless of whether we stumble or strut home, and tackles us with delight because we are his. We are his and we are holy, hairs out of place and broken hearts too.

Last night, I watched you sit cross-legged on the bed across from me and detail your day. Your long blond hair hung down like Rapunzel's over your shoulder and you laughed big, mouth open wide and two front teeth large and lovely, like your mother's. I suddenly caught a glimpse of you, all elbows and knees, at twelve or thirteen, and it took my breath away. How is it that you exist? That by some miracle I get to help write the story of your life? It stuns me.

This love I feel for you, Lucy? It is but a shadow of the love of God. In your life, the world—and even the church—is going to tell you a lot of half-truths about who God is and what God's about, so I want to lay the groundwork here and now for whatever is to come. You were created by, with, and for the purpose of love. That is the identity of Christ. Follow him, and the freedom of a life well-lived will follow. It might not be an easy life; in fact, we have the assurance that it will be hard, and often. But when you trust in Jesus to provide, he will.

Jesus will strengthen your spirit in times of weakness, give you bold authority to cast out lies and nonsense, and delight you with surprises. There will be times when you wonder if you're getting this faith thing "right," and let me dispel that notion for you now: you aren't. This is good. If we got all the answers right, there would be no need for Jesus, and without Jesus there is no point. He is the Friend who comforts, the Lover who knows you, the Parent who guides you, the Savior who redeems you. There is not a single sin, or victory, outside of his reach. So hold fast to him. The "good," ordered life is nice for a while, but you will long for more. You will want a wild adventure and you will find it in Jesus. Calling him your King will cost you at times—cost you popularity, certainty, relationships; political, professional, or personal power; and even, perhaps, your life—but it will never be boring, and it will never, ever leave you less than it found you. That's what religion can do sometimes. That's what the world does.

"But take heart!" Jesus said. "I have overcome the world" (John 16:33).

You will make mistakes, and you will sin. You will try and fail, and I hope you'll try again. You will believe one thing about faith and change your mind later. You will wonder if all of this is even worth the effort.

Maybe not, but Jesus is. Trust your mother on this one. Every time I thought I knew it all, Jesus showed me a new horizon. Every time I thought I'd gone too far, Jesus carried me home.

Take heart, Lucy. And remember, life doesn't have to be perfect to be good.

I love you.

Mom

CHAPTER 19

Good Enough

A few weeks before I left to go to college, I attended a small Bible study with a dear friend from high school.
He was home for the summer from an intense discipleship training program in California, and as I prepped to leave home for the first time, I relied on his friendship, as I had in high school, to help ground my faith. I sensed that my views on God would change in college—an idea that concerned me—and I agreed to attend the Bible study with my friend as a final girding against any spiritual attack that might come my way.

That night, I showed up to the study with a downtrodden soul. It's fair to say that while I walked into that room with a smile and a well-worn Bible, my spirit trudged in with crossed arms and a cocked eyebrow. I was nursing a heartbreak in addition to my concerns about God, and was only there because I thought it was the right thing to do, not because I was excited to be in community with other believers.

Over the course of a few hours, I listened to the testimonies of people my age—some of whom I knew from school and some of whom were strangers—about how Jesus had challenged and changed them. These were the kinds of stories I had heard only from the friend who invited me there, and my spirit perked up as I listened to what God had accomplished in their lives. No one said anything extraordinary, but their sheer joy in knowing Jesus was an odd and transformative departure from the norm. They didn't seem to just love and want to follow Jesus; they also appeared to like him. Huh.

The old and tired version of God—the God who stayed happy as long as I read my Bible and prayed and didn't act a fool—gave way to a fresh and relevant one, a God with a deep and abiding love for me—Wendi—specifically. In a summer that had been marked by both the sting of rejection and excitement about the future, this was good news. This was the Good News.

At dinner afterward, I babbled on with enthusiasm about what I'd felt in that Bible study. My friend listened with an expression of delight, and I wondered if maybe he had hoped something like this would happen. Back at my house, he encouraged me to go inside and spend some time in prayer to see what God would reveal as I prepared to make the transition from home to a university four hours away.

In my bedroom, I opened my Bible on the floor and bent over it, eager to hear from God. I prayed with earnest for him to show me what I needed to know, to help me find footing as I walked toward a thrilling, unknown, future. I opened to a random page in Matthew and began to read: "Therefore everyone who hears these words of mine and puts them into practice is like a wise man who built his house on the rock. The rain came down, the streams rose, and the winds blew and beat against that house; yet it did not fall, because it had its foundation on the rock" (Matt. 7:24–25).

One of my favorite podcast hosts often asks her guests how they hear from God. I hear from him in words and phrases that interrupt my own line of thinking with a gentle shift in direction or a repeated affirmation that I'm headed the right way. There is an interior pressing that accompanies these words, a spiritual firm hand that can sometimes be as obvious as a physical one. It never goes away until I begin to act on what I hear. There have been a few rare moments in my faith walk when I feel like the Spirit kicks me in the pants. This was one of those times.

I was overjoyed about going to college, but I had never been to a party or had sex or done much of anything worth gossiping about except all those times I fooled around with my high school boyfriend in the band room. (Sorry, Mr. Ridley.) I had never wanted to do much of anything worth gossiping about until right before I left for university. Suddenly, I realized I was about to leave the built-in security of my parents and lifelong community for a big, wide world where no one was in charge of me anymore except . . . me. Who was I, really? Who would I become on my own, with no one around to tether me to the rules?

This verse in Matthew became my life verse, and I jumped into friendships, classes, parties, and romance with a faith swagger like the one I had in high school, but on steroids. I was a kind and loving friend, loyal to a fault, but I repeatedly put my foot in my mouth. It wasn't enough that my friends came to me for advice; I felt compelled to fix their lives. To fix them. Faith was a tool for behavior modification, and because the rules had kept me safe for so long, I presented them to my friends and loved ones as the standard to which they should conform. I longed for them to feel safe the way I did, to know that God had big plans for their lives. I thought the rules were the answer and overlooked Jesus entirely.

Sometime in the middle of my university years, I became acutely aware that the people most dear to me were often not the ones who behaved like I did. They were the people who showed up for me, who asked hard questions, and even gave me shit about my rigid adherence to the moral conventions of my evangelical faith.

I learned to listen more. I held my tongue when I saw the need for a hug instead. I released my grip on perfection one finger at a time and tasted real freedom in the form of relationships. I discovered I was not the teacher, nor had anyone asked me to be. I was the student, and

God made himself known to me through his children. God nurtured community in me over chips and salsa at El Sombrero, blessed me with rest in nights sprawled across the couch in my friend's apartment, showed me mercy in tearful conversations as Jack's Mannequin played in the background, and offered me joy in hilarious games of beer pong between study sessions.

With the love of friends, God saved me from a university experience marked by a clear but very lonely conscience. My life verse hadn't been wrong, but I had viewed it with obscure vision. God had wanted more for me than right living and superior morality. He had wanted me to know, and love, people. He had wanted me to know and love him.

●　·　·　●●●　　　　·
●　　·　　●

The little girl who admired her parents and loved her God, the young woman who wanted to live without regret, the new mom who carried so much fear about how to do things the right way . . . all of these people exist within me still. We are never just one person, but a hundred over a lifetime, if we're lucky.

The gratitude I feel for the faith instilled in me as a child is unmatched. It has been the home base from which I felt safe to explore. God, being the Good Parent that he is, leaned into his daughter while I grabbed for easy pieces of him to chart a path as best I could. He was patient and accommodating, sometimes quiet, other times as loud as Aslan's roar, but always near. Always present.

In those early morning postpartum days, as I wrestled with God from our back porch, God kept me suspended. I had nothing new from which to glean my hope, so I held fast to what I had seen God do and what I knew about his character.

One morning, I asked God why I didn't see the cardinals anymore. The heat of the summer cocooned me like a warm blanket even before dawn, so why didn't I hear their calls as the sun rose through the branches? Perhaps they'd had enough of my tears. I sure had. I told God I wanted to see him, to believe he was still there. I was specific with my request. Could he let the cardinals out again and remind me of when I was happy, of early afternoons spent exploring with Lucy, of a waiting season that had brought forth life? I prayed, sat still, and looked all around the yard—up in the trees, across the grass, on top of the fence. Nothing. I did this for two days.

On the third day, I didn't ask again. I drank my coffee and then pressed my forehead to my knees, sleep still close by but unattainable now that my brain had woken up. With my eyes closed, I took deep breaths and imagined pushing my obsessions out with the air in my lungs. In come the intrusive thoughts, out go the lies. In, out. In, out. I tasted the coffee on my tongue as I breathed and felt safe with my head tucked inside my arms like a makeshift turtle shell.

Then came the song. "Pur-ty, pur-ty, pur-ty," it trilled.

My head snapped up at the sound, and I saw it then, a large, red-breasted male perched still and stately atop the fence closest to me. It peered in my direction and cocked its head as a rush of emotions coursed through my body, making me lightheaded. I scoffed in disbelief at what I was seeing.

"Hi," I said in a small voice.

The cardinal looked at me for another moment and then flew away. I gathered my thoughts and sat frozen to the steps as the minutes passed. "Thank you," I said to the quiet morning air, to the Spirit in my soul.

I wish I could tell you I healed quickly after my interlude with the cardinal, but God is not a magician. He could have taken away my pain with less than a word. He has done it for people before and I'm sure he will do it again. This has not been my experience with suffering, but it doesn't make the healing that has come any less miraculous. I was on the brink of death and Love rescued me, one day, one meal, one conversation at a time.

Love rescued me with messages from friends, family, and strangers alike, who cared for me with candles and books and coffee and prayers.

Love rescued me with caretakers who entertained and watched over my children and reminded me to nourish my body.

Love rescued me with words from childhood friends who understood my pain, who had been through such darkness themselves.

Love rescued me with a husband who spoke truth to my anxious mind and lived out the words he spoke so long ago now, in sickness and in health.

Love rescued me with a small-town doctor who paid attention—twice—and a counselor who honored all the mixed-up, wonderful parts of me.

Love rescued me with work and a regular schedule again.

Love rescued me with Zoloft.

Love rescued me with time.

"For the one whom God has sent speaks the words of God, for God gives the Spirit without limit" (John 3:34). When Love moves, it moves wherever—and through whomever—it requires.

The point, really, is not even how Love rescued me, but that it did. In rescuing me, Love also rescued my daughter, my son, and my husband. And it will again. This is what Jesus does best. Sometimes, the beauty from the ashes is not a grandiose new understanding of the world or even a fresh sense of purpose, but simply this: That you survived the fire and lived to tell about it. That you came to a place where performance did not matter and the flames had burned away all that kept you from what was truly, powerfully good.

As it turns out, my friend was right. God wasn't silent; God was speaking to me all along, but not in a whole new way as we had suspected. He was speaking the way he has since I was a little girl who wanted to know and obey the Lord, since I was a young adult who wanted to be victorious in faith, since I became a mother and discovered a whole new set of fears about how to be good in life.

Through his delivered, redeemed people. His imperfect, wonky, sometimes wrong, but always holy people.

Before we go our separate ways, I want to encourage you that work is not what saves us. Our works are what point people to Jesus. How we live our lives, what we choose to do with the time and energy we've been given no matter what stage of life we're in, is not what Jesus requires to love or redeem us. No, what Jesus requires is that we love him and love others well so our lives will both glorify him and show people the way to eternity. The way to love, to wholeness, to holiness. Our salvation is fixed the moment we choose to follow Christ, yes, but our sanctification is a lifelong process. It's progress, day by day, moment by moment.

And, as my friend Cailyn says, progress is better than perfection.

We need not look at the progress as drudgery, though, simply because it might have been that way in the past. It's not always going to be fun or easy to make choices that reflect God's position in our lives, as I'm sure you well know, and those choices, while certainly challenging, need not stifle us. As any parent knows, freedom thrives where we set limits and trust our children to move within them. Those limits should build trust, but—and here's a distinction I need you to see—not in our own abilities. Of course, we should take pride in the choices that lead us to light and truth and beauty, but we must recognize what, or rather who, equipped us with the tools needed to make those choices. It is God's faithfulness that guards and guides us, and that's why we don't have to be afraid of failure. That's why we don't need to pursue perfection. Our Creator is fully aware that we can't do it without him, and he's not waiting on you to fall apart. God is eagerly keeping watch over you with the same kind of tenderness you offer your own babies.

My friend, the standard set before us is Christ. It is not the law, nor is it our often misinterpretation of the law. And our Savior will be faithful in his promise to transform us into his likeness.

Let me repeat that: Christ will be faithful in his promise to transform us.

It was his promise made, so it will be his promise fulfilled. It's not a journey left up to us alone. It's not a path we must follow perfectly in order to reach the destination he has in mind. I know full well what it looks like to run the race alone and go tumbling over my own feet, and it's not a race I want to run again.

In *The Weight of Glory*, C. S. Lewis takes our misguided pursuits to task when he says:

It would seem that Our Lord finds our desires not too strong, but too weak. We are half-hearted creatures, fooling about with drink and sex and ambition when infinite joy is offered us, like an ignorant child who wants to go on making mud pies in a slum because he cannot imagine what is meant by the offer of a holiday at the sea. We are far too easily pleased.

I fooled about not with drink or sex but with the idea of perfection. I made mud pies filled with my own pride and all the good things I had accomplished, and Jesus invited me to gently set all that aside and come away with him for a holiday at sea, for a life full of joy and righteousness not dependent on my behavior or perfect thoughts but on his sacrifice.

Your work is not needed so you can earn your place alongside the Savior. Your work is necessary because it is an act of faith each time you choose obedience, and when you approach it with that mindset, you're only going to experience God more deeply. I wrote this book because after my decades of serving him with good deeds, the Lord allowed me to walk through impenetrable darkness and used it to completely transform my heart. He used my pain to highlight how deeply I had misunderstood both his character and his love, and I do not want to keep quiet about that. It rescued me from a lifetime of self-serving rightness and introduced me to the richness of Jesus. And, you guys, Jesus is it. When you get Jesus, you get everything. You get to put aside the mud pies and steal away for a holiday at sea. Perhaps that holiday is different from what you expected; mine certainly has been. But I would not trade it. Because of the way the Lord moved through the darkness of my heart, whatever I thought was light before has been proven to be little more than shadow.

Even if you're already a Jesus follower, the invitation remains. This could be the moment you accept his invitation for the first time. Your salvation has already been secured, but perhaps now your life will start to reflect the faith you put in him, rather than the stability you've been seeking through performance.

My friend, it is for freedom that Christ has set you free. The freedom to unfollow, cancel, or otherwise delete from your life the things that try to trap you in the bondage of perfection. The freedom to boldly declare your weakness and call on the Spirit to bring forth fruit from the ashes of whatever needed to burn. The freedom to delight in goodness and wisdom without the guilt of still needing help. The freedom to let go of perfection because you have already been made holy.

The ink is already dry on the page. Your name is there, waiting to be read, on the day you begin eternity. And do you know what's written next to it? The words Jesus has been declaring over you since the very moment you met him.

Good.

Enough.

ACKNOWLEDGMENTS

Dear Reader, I sincerely hope you take the time to read these acknowledgments because it's the whole and honest truth that no book finds its way out into the world without a bunch of wonderful people coming together to make it happen.

First, to Jon, Michelle, Rachel, Jennifer, and everyone at Paraclete Press for believing in this book. You helped turn an idea into something worth reading, and I am forever grateful that you took a chance on me. Thank you.

To Jonathan Merritt, for being such a kind human to a writer he'd only just met.

To Meade, for your counsel and constant encouragement over this last, wild year.

To Dr. William Parrish, for being a fantastic physician and a fantastic person.

To my podcast listeners, email subscribers, and internet friends, thank you for sending light and love to this project along the way. People buy books because they trust readers who love them, and you guys have loved me—and my work—well.

To my Thursday Church, past and present, for being the best cheerleaders, challengers, and iron sharpeners I have ever known. So many of the lessons I wrote about in this book I learned with you. I love you so.

To my beloved family and friends—of which I am grateful to have many—who stood by me when life felt close to the edge and stand beside me still. Every unexpected gift in the mail, every text, every call, every shared story, and every moment given pulled me back from the precipice. I am still here because of your love.

To my Mom and Dad for giving me what every person deserves: a happy childhood and a safe place to come home to, no matter how that home changes along the way. You are the foundation of every story in this book, the cornerstone of all that is good in my life. I hope you always know how much I honor and adore you both.

To Pierce. Always Pierce. In this case, words just really aren't enough. What a joy it has been to share this life with you, to walk through all that we have together. You embody grace and love, for me and for our children. We are the luckiest. I am the luckiest.

To Lucy and Theo, my light and my gift. You both shine with such ferocity and joy that it stuns me. Being your mother is a delight and a salvation of its own kind.

And to the One who made me holy and calls me good, over and over again. I will never be able to thank You enough.

ABOUT PARACLETE PRESS

Who We Are

As the publishing arm of the Community of Jesus, Paraclete Press presents a full expression of Christian belief and practice—from Catholic to Evangelical, from Protestant to Orthodox, reflecting the ecumenical charism of the Community and its dedication to sacred music, the fine arts, and the written word. We publish books, recordings, sheet music, and video/DVDs that nourish the vibrant life of the church and its people.

What We Are Doing

BOOKS | PARACLETE PRESS BOOKS show the richness and depth of what it means to be Christian. While Benedictine spirituality is at the heart of who we are and all that we do, our books reflect the Christian experience across many cultures, time periods, and houses of worship.

We have many series, including *Paraclete Essentials*; *Paraclete Fiction*; *Paraclete Poetry*; *Paraclete Giants*; and for children and adults, *All God's Creatures*, books about animals and faith; and *San Damiano Books*, focusing on Franciscan spirituality. Others include *Voices from the Monastery* (men and women monastics writing about living a spiritual life today), *Active Prayer*, and new for young readers: *The Pope's Cat*. We also specialize in gift books for children on the occasions of Baptism and First Communion, as well as other important times in a child's life, and books that bring creativity and liveliness to any adult spiritual life.

The MOUNT TABOR BOOKS series focuses on the arts and literature as well as liturgical worship and spirituality; it was created in conjunction with the Mount Tabor Ecumenical Centre for Art and Spirituality in Barga, Italy.

MUSIC | PARACLETE PRESS DISTRIBUTES RECORDINGS of the internationally acclaimed choir *Gloriæ Dei Cantores*, the *Gloriæ Dei Cantores Schola*, and the other instrumental artists of the *Arts Empowering Life Foundation*.

PARACLETE PRESS IS THE EXCLUSIVE NORTH AMERICAN DISTRIBUTOR for the Gregorian chant recordings from St. Peter's Abbey in Solesmes, France. Paraclete also carries all of the Solesmes chant publications for Mass and the Divine Office, as well as their academic research publications.

In addition, PARACLETE PRESS SHEET MUSIC publishes the work of today's finest composers of sacred choral music, annually reviewing over 1,000 works and releasing between 40 and 60 works for both choir and organ.

VIDEO | Our video/DVDs offer spiritual help, healing, and biblical guidance for a broad range of life issues including grief and loss, marriage, forgiveness, facing death, understanding suicide, bullying, addictions, Alzheimer's, and Christian formation.

Learn more about us at our website
www.paracletepress.com
or phone us toll-free at 1.800.451.5006

SCAN
TO
READ

YOU MAY ALSO BE INTERESTED IN . . .

Glory Happening
Finding the Divine in Everyday Places

KAITLIN B. CURTICE

ISBN 978-1-61261-896-9
Trade paperback | $16.99

"With the insights of a prophet and the attention of a poet, Kaitlin Curtice invites the reader to see the world fresh, in all its everyday glory. You will never look at a sink of dishes, a mound of dough, a game of Rummy, or the family dog the same way again. A stunner of a debut, every sentence a feast for the senses."—**Rachel Held Evans**

Everbloom
Stories of Deeply Rooted and Transformed Lives

Women of Redbud Writers Guild

ISBN 978-1-61261-933-0
Trade paperback | $17.99

"We read to see elements of our own hearts, experiences and stories reflected back to us in the words of others. This collection is just that: stories that help us feel seen, known, and understood. Honestly and beautifully told, this book will keep you in good company along your own journey."—**Shauna Niequist**

Flunking Sainthood
A Year of Breaking the Sabbath, Forgetting to Pray, and Still Loving My Neighbor

JANA RIESS

ISBN 978-1-55725-660-7
Trade paperback | $16.99

"*Flunking Sainthood* is surprising and freeing; it is fun and funny; and it is full of wisdom. It is, in fact, the best book on the practices of the spiritual life that I have read in a long, long time."—**Lauren Winner**